MW00974032

My Son, If You Accept My Words

SONDRA LEE

WESTBOW
PRESS®
A DIVISION OF THOMAS NELSON
& ZONDERVAN

This book is a work of non-fiction. Unless otherwise noted, the author
and the publisher make no explicit guarantees as to the accuracy of
the information contained in this book and in some cases, names of
people and places have been altered to protect their privacy.

WestBow Press books may be ordered through booksellers or by contacting:

WestBow Press
A Division of Thomas Nelson & Zondervan
1663 Liberty Drive
Bloomington, IN 47403
www.westbowpress.com
1 (866) 928-1240

Because of the dynamic nature of the Internet, any web addresses or
links contained in this book may have changed since publication and
may no longer be valid. The views expressed in this work are solely those
of the author and do not necessarily reflect the views of the publisher,
and the publisher hereby disclaims any responsibility for them.

Scripture quotations taken from the King James Version of the Bible.

ISBN: 978-1-9736-7518-1 (sc)
ISBN: 978-1-9736-7519-8 (hc)
ISBN: 978-1-9736-7517-4 (e)

Library of Congress Control Number: 2019914607

Print information available on the last page.

WestBow Press rev. date: 9/26/2019

To my only son,
Tristan.
With all my love,
Mommy

Acknowledgments

I want to thank the Lord Jesus Christ, my Savior, for saving my soul at twelve years old and for being my source of hope, strength, and comfort throughout my life. Without the Lord, I could not have written this book. Without the Lord, I would not have been so blessed with this abundant life of motherhood and would not have hope for either my future or my son's future in order to write this book with His plan and purpose in mind. "The joy of the Lord is [my] strength" (Nehemiah 8:10).

I want to thank my wonderful, supportive husband, who makes me feel like I can accomplish anything that I set my mind to do. He lets me know that he has full confidence in me, and I am eternally grateful. Without him, I would be a mess. The Lord truly gave me what I needed in him.

I want to thank my son, Tristan, who inspired me to write this book. Throughout his childhood I was blessed to witness his love for others, his belief in others, and his pure heart toward the world. This beautiful young love and naivete is what motivated me in the beginning of this journey to write this book. I want nothing but the best for him, my dear son. His heart has always filled me with joy. I am so grateful to have been entrusted with him as my son. The Lord opened my heart to a love that I didn't know existed until his birth. He made us a family, and I am eternally grateful.

I want to thank my daughter, Lydia, who has supported this endeavor and has wanted nothing but the best for her mommy while I have poured my heart out onto paper. She has sacrificed time and has been my cheerleader throughout this endeavor. I am so grateful for her gift of love, which she shows me on a daily basis. I am eternally grateful for the gift of her sweet heart to cherish each and every day. She has made our family complete. My joy is full.

I want to thank my mother. I have been so richly blessed by her mothering and her sacrificial giving throughout my entire life. She always believes in me and thinks I can do anything. I am so thankful to have a mother who was and continues to be the best example of unconditional love I could have ever hoped for.

I want to thank my pastor, Brother Greg Butler, for being the most humble, caring, and sincere pastor I could have ever hoped for, for our family. He is truly a shepherd to his flock. He cares about his congregation. He honors the Lord with his teaching and preaching. He relays the messages that the Lord places in his heart to meet the needs of his congregation while unapologetically sharing the truth of the Bible. With all his responsibilities, he chose to help me with this project. I could not have completed this book without his counsel and encouragement. I thank the Lord for having a pastor who loves and cares the way he does.

I want to thank Brother Don Richards and Brother Tommy Foskey for being true Christians in my formative years. These men allowed me to witness a different way of life. I saw in them the answer I had been seeking in my own life. I had attended church alone through different bus ministries throughout my childhood. When I was twelve years old, the Lord led our family to Corinth Baptist Church, where I was miraculously saved during a revival led by Evangelist J. Harold Smith. For the first time in my life, our family began to attend church together. No matter what life was like at home, I could see that these men were different. They were sincere and had the Truth. The impact they have made on my life is more than I can express. All I can say is, Thank you for being used by the Lord, for I am a life that was impacted, changed, and made new. Thank you for sharing Jesus not only in your speech but also in the way you live.

I also want to thank Brother Mack Waters for being a godly example of a man who lived his life to the fullest to the very end. He encouraged me to do my best for the Lord. He always said, "Do your best, and He will bless." I appreciate his love for me and my family. The godly heritage that he left for his family is what I desire for my own family. I thank the Lord for the years that I was able to witness his undying faith and devotion to our Lord Jesus Christ and to his family.

Lastly, I want to thank three ladies who have taught me what true friendship means.

My friend Traci is the most loving, tenderhearted serving Christian I have ever encountered. Thank you for being my heart friend. You always claim the Lord's promises and hold onto hope. You exude love. You hope all things, believe all things, and endure all things. Your friendship is truly a treasure to my heart.

My friend Patricia, who is an example of unconditional love, is a friend through the mountaintops and valleys of life. Thank you, Patricia, for fasting and praying with me for my precious son. The Lord has used you in a mighty way in my life. I will always be grateful for your presence in my life. You always point others to the Word. You are a gift.

And my dear friend Susan, I cannot thank the Lord enough for giving me a friend like you. He has blessed me with a kindred spirit in you. You are a like-minded friend indeed and a friend who always says, "What can I do?" You are a confidant who is filled with His truth. I appreciate you so very much. Thank you for your love and care in my life.

The Lord has used each of these people to bless my heart with encouragement and to heal my heart in ways of which they are unaware. The Lord has been so very good, and I am so very thankful. "Without Him, I could do nothing. Without Him, I'd surely fail. Without Him, I would be drifting, like a ship without a sail."[1]

---

[1] Mylon LeFevre, "Without Him" (hymn), 1963.

Preface

Proverbs 2

My son, if thou wilt receive my words, and hide my commandments with thee; So that thou incline thine ear unto wisdom, and apply thine heart to understanding; Yea, if thou criest after knowledge, and liftest up thy voice for understanding; If thou seekest her as silver, and searchest for her as for hid treasures; Then shalt thou understand the fear of the Lord, and find the knowledge of God. For the Lord giveth wisdom: out of his mouth cometh knowledge and understanding. He layeth up sound wisdom for the righteous: he is a buckler to them that walk uprightly. He keepeth the paths of judgment, and preserveth the way of his saints. Then shalt thou understand righteousness, and judgment, and equity; yea, every good path. When wisdom entereth into thine heart, and knowledge is pleasant unto thy soul; Discretion shall preserve thee, understanding shall keep thee: To deliver thee from the way of the evil man. (Proverbs 2:1–12)

Happy is the man that findeth wisdom, and the man that getteth understanding. (Proverbs 2:13)

What is more profitable than silver? What yields
better return than gold? What is more precious
than rubies? What is not comparable to anything
else that you can desire? What has long life in her
right hand? What has riches and honor in her left
hand? Whose ways are pleasant ways, and whose
paths are filled with peace? Who is she that is a
tree of life to those who embrace her? Those who
retaineth her will be blessed. (Proverbs 3:13–20)

My son, who is she?
She is wisdom.

"Happy is the man who findeth wisdom, and the
man that getteth understanding" (Proverbs 3:13).

How do you find wisdom? By hiding the Lord's Word in
your heart. May you accept His teachings, apply His Word to
your life, and allow your heart, soul, and mind to be filled with
His understanding and discretion. These are two qualities that
can only be attained because you receive, accept, and apply His
instruction to your life.

I pray right now, Son, that you will be that man. My prayer is
that you will seek wisdom all your life and that you will remain
humble enough throughout all your days to know that no matter
how much wisdom you have acquired, there is always more to be
learned and applied to your life. Never forget the days of learning
so that you will be patient with others as they too seek to grow
and learn.[2] Be a man of wisdom.

This book is written for my precious son, Tristan. He has been
and always will be a joy to my heart. *The Lord placed the desire*

<hr>

[2] Warren Wiersbe, *Bible Commentary: Old Testament* (Nashville: Thomas
Nelson, 2000).

in my heart to write this book in order to help guide, enable, and lead my only son to the making of wise choices in his life. I cannot impart wisdom and discernment, but I can, through the study of God's Word and through prayer, place my hope in the Lord, in His complete and sovereign ability, trust that He will impart His wisdom to this precious gift that has been entrusted to me. I pray that the reading of each devotion in *My Son, if You Accept My Words* will be preceded by prayer and petition for wisdom and discernment. Please meditate on the verses and commit your ways to Him. My prayer for you, my son, is, "Then I commended mirth, because a man hath no better thing under the sun, than to eat, and to drink, and to be merry: for that shall abide with him of his labour the days of his life, which God giveth him under the sun" (Ecclesiastes 8:15).

Introduction

I originally wrote *My Son, if You Accept My Words* for my son and for him alone. I was burdened by the beautiful naivete that he displayed in his heart toward others when he was a young teenager. As I began writing, the Lord burdened my heart for the many other young men in our lives. Their mothers and I have been on this mothering journey together for years. We have been bonded by friendship and a love for each other's children. As these friends learned of this book I was writing, they began to ask me if I would make it available to them to give to their sons. After much prayer, seeking of counsel, and confirmation, I have been led to make *My Son, if You Accept My Words* available to anyone who is seeking a resource for young men to study God's Word and see the practical application of His Word in their own lives, which will hopefully help equip them to make wise decisions for their future. May each chapter be preceded by prayer for wisdom and discernment. May the Lord use *My Son, if You Accept My Words* to open the hearts and eyes of our young men to their calling to be leaders, warriors, and servants. May each young man see the need in his own life to "be … therefore wise as serpents, and harmless as doves" (Matthew 10:16). It is my prayer that every young man who chooses to read *My Son, if You Accept My Words* will read it as though his own mother is speaking to him.

Dearest Son,

I write this book to help you to know what God wants for you in your life. I know completely that it is not me who imparts wisdom, but only the Lord may impart wisdom and discernment. But knowing that I have been entrusted with you to raise for His glory, I believe that it is my duty to share what God has laid on my heart and what He has taught me throughout the trials of my own life. I want to give you all the tools necessary to make wise decisions. *I hope and pray that after reading this book, you will see how practical God's Word is in our everyday lives and in the decisions we make, both big and small.*

Son, one of my hopes in writing this book is that you won't find yourself later in life like Solomon. He was the wisest man here on earth, yet he found himself at the end of his life compromising the truths he knew in his heart because of the pagan hearts of the women he had entangled himself with. Son, we can never be so prideful as to think that we could not fall into the same trap. There is a lady whom the Lord has set aside just for you, one who He knows will be the perfect helpmeet for you. The Lord has a plan and a purpose for your life. This plan for you will bring you peace and not evil all the days of your life (Jeremiah 29:11). My prayer is that you will not settle for anything less than His best. There may be many good options, but there is only one right choice. The only right choice is what God has set out for you. I have prayed for your future spouse since you were a baby. My prayer is (1) that she loves the Lord with all her heart, strength, and mind, (2) that she is trustworthy, sincere, and kind, (3) that she is filled with mercy, (4) that she will love you with all her heart and will look out for your best interests, (5) that she will raise your children and teach them diligently to love the Lord with all their hearts, (6) that she will raise your children to honor the Lord with their lives and to honor you, (7) that she will bless you in everything the two of you do, and (8) that she will love you with her whole heart and you will be able to have full confidence in her (Proverbs 31:11) to do what is true and right inside and outside your home.

My sweet son, it has been and is the most wonderful opportunity of responsibility to be your mother. I cherish every moment I have had and every moment I will be given to love, nurture, and train you. As I have always said, you are truly a joy to my heart. I want nothing but the best for you in your life. Remember, the best is not always the easy way, for His ways are not our ways. Commit your way to Him, and He will direct your path. No matter what, Son, the Lord is there with His arms open wide, wanting fellowship with you. Honor Him in everything you do. As Brother Mack Waters often said, "Do your best, and He will bless!" The Lord's timing is not our timing. Sometimes we don't see His best in a situation until later or even after we die, but the only thing we are to do is to trust and obey. "These all died in faith, not having received the promises, but having seen them afar off, and were persuaded of them, and embraced them, and confessed that they were strangers and pilgrims on the earth" (Hebrews 11:13).

Dear son, I pray that your life be filled with His joy and His mercies. I love you with all my heart.

Love,

Mommy

CHAPTER 1

Ruth

Dear Son,

    As you read this chapter concerning Ruth, please consider in light of marriage how important it is to *be* the right person and not just to *find* the right person. Another important fact to consider is that all the events described in the book of Ruth took place during a time when conditions were less than ideal. It was a very dark time in history, yet the Lord found two people honoring Him with their lives to the best of their ability. This was a time described as such: "Those days there was no king in Israel: every man did that which was right in his own eyes" (Judges 21:25). No matter what the state of the world is in, if you are serving the Lord, He will fulfill His purposes for your life. You just need to continue to do your best so that He can bless you. "For the eyes of the Lord run to and fro throughout the whole earth, to shew himself strong in the behalf of them whose heart is perfect toward him" (2 Chronicles 16:9a). I believe the Lord is still looking to and fro for someone to show himself strong. I believe He is still looking for people whose hearts are fully committed to Him. Be that one, my son. Be a blessing to Him in all that you do.

Ruth 1

> Now it came to pass in the days when the judges ruled, that there was a famine in the land. And a certain man of Bethlehemjudah went to sojourn in the country of Moab, he, and his wife, and his two sons. And the name of the man was Elimelech, and the name of his wife Naomi, and the name of his two sons Mahlon and Chilion, Ephrathites of Bethlehemjudah. And they came into the country of Moab, and continued there. And Elimelech Naomi's husband died; and she was left, and her two sons. And they took them wives of the women of Moab; the name of the one was Orpah, and the name of the other Ruth: and they dwelled there about ten years. And Mahlon and Chilion died also both of them; and the woman was left of her two sons and her husband. (Ruth 1:1–5)

We can learn a great deal from this one chapter. It is better to be hungry and be in the will of God than to have a full stomach and be out of His will. A famine came upon the land. Elimelech, being a father and husband, wanted to protect his family from this famine. Instead of trusting in the Lord to provide, he relied on his own decision to remedy the situation. He took his wife and two sons to live for "a while" in the country of Moab. All sin starts out with "It will only be for a little while." Always remember, partial obedience is complete disobedience. He did not think his intention to stay for a little while in the enemy's country would cost so much. Again, sin will take you farther than you want to go, keep you longer than you want to stay, and cost you more than you are willing to pay. Elimilech and his wife planned to stay in Moab a short time, but their "sojourn" lasted long enough for their sons to marry. The Lord is giving us an example of the father's sin falling upon his children. Elimilech did not foresee the implications of his sin of moving into enemy territory, thus his sons did not think it to be a sin to entangle themselves in marriage to enemy foreign wives. Their father did not see the magnitude of his disobedience, and neither did they. He reasoned out why they should make the move, and they reasoned why they should each marry a Moabite. I imagine his sons used the same reasoning and rationalizing of their sin of entangling themselves with the enemy as Elimilech had used, thinking to themselves, *God will not punish us for marrying Moabite women. These are the only women we may choose from in this land of Moab. God wants us to marry and be fruitful and multiply, so He will not punish us if we marry the only women available to us.* This is the same "logic" that Elimilech displayed in his decision to move. *There is no food here, so we need to move. God will not punish me for providing for my family. I am called to be the provider. How can I provide if I do not move to enemy territory, where there is food available?* Neither father nor son sought the Lord or waited on the Lord.

Sometimes we are called to do things that do not make sense. Circumstances come up that immediately make us look to ourselves, but the Lord wants us to trust in Him, rely on Him, depend on Him, allow Him to provide, and allow Him to grow our faith. These types of circumstances test our faithfulness. Are we willing to trust in Him to provide? Obedience to the Lord requires self-discipline and sacrifice. We must be willing to seek out His truth in a matter. If Elimilech and his sons would have sought wisdom from God's Word, they would have found the following command: "An Ammonite or Moabite shall not enter into the congregation of the Lord; even to their tenth generation shall they not enter into the congregation of the Lord forever" (Deuteronomy 23:3). Elimilech and his family lived in enemy territory for ten years. Elimilech was the head of the household. He was charged with the responsibility to know and seek what was best for his family. He should have known the law, obeyed the commands, and sought the Lord. If he would have sought wisdom and applied God's Word to his life, he would have known that even though there was a famine, he and his family were not excused to go live in enemy territory. With this information, he would have been equipped to make the right decision to lead his family to remain faithful, even during times of famine. His sons would have had the opportunity to witness the discipline of waiting on the Lord. They would have learned to trust in His sovereignty during trials and tribulations, and they would have seen the blessings that come from the act of obeying at all costs. Can you imagine how different all our lives would be if each husband and father took his role seriously enough to seek wisdom, study the Word, and apply it to his decision-making for his family? The ripple effect would be tremendous!

The consequence of their sin was not immediate, but it was sure: both Elimilech and his sons died. You can run away from famine, but you cannot escape the wages of sin, which is death.

> Then she arose with her daughters in law, that she might return from the country of Moab: for she had heard in the country of Moab how that the Lord had visited his people in giving them bread.

Wherefore she went forth out of the place where she was, and her two daughters in law with her; and they went on the way to return unto the land of Judah. And Naomi said unto her two daughters in law, Go, return each to her mother's house: the Lord deal kindly with you, as ye have dealt with the dead, and with me. The Lord grant you that ye may find rest, each of you in the house of her husband. Then she kissed them; and they lifted up their voice, and wept. And they said unto her, Surely we will return with thee unto thy people. (Ruth 1:6–10)

In verse 6, while Naomi was still residing in enemy territory, she learned that the Lord had come to the aid of His people. After living in Moab for ten years, Naomi prepared to return home. Even though this passage does not say that Elimelech's or his family's faith had weakened, we see by their actions that their devotion to Him faltered once they started relying on their own strength and not on His strength.

Naomi is such a picture of love.

"Wherefore she went forth out of the place where she was, and her two daughters in law with her; and they went on the way to return unto the land of Judah. And Naomi said unto her two daughters in law, Go, return each to her mother's house: the Lord deal kindly with you, as ye have dealt with the dead, and with me. The Lord grant you that ye may find rest, each of you in the house of her husband" (Ruth 1:7–9). What a loving mother-in-law. She truly loved those women. She displayed a sincere interest in their well-being. She was concerned about what would be best for them. She knew they would be rejected by those in Judah because they were the "enemy." She desired to protect them from further pain and urged them to go back to their home country of Moab. She prayed that the Lord's blessings would be upon them, and she wanted them to find rest. She was not self-centered. Naomi was no longer worried about suffering through yet another famine in her life but was willing to face the consequences of her family's sin alone. Her love for her daughters-in-law and her desire to go back to the land of Judah is evident for she knew her sovereign Lord is the rescuer, protector, and provider during famine. "Then she kissed them; and they lifted up their voice, and wept. And they said unto her, Surely we will return with thee unto thy people" (Ruth 1:9b–10).

Naomi—what a picture of faith she is. In her deepest hour of need, she still sought that which was good for her daughters-in-law. She had lost both her husband and her children and did not turn against the Lord, but she recognized His sovereignty. She said, "For the Almighty hath dealt very bitterly with me." The Lord dealt with her bitterly, but she was not bitter. She was still seeking to serve her daughters-in-law, was still serving others. Her relationship with her daughters-in-law obviously was not solely based on their relationship with her sons. She had established trust and a covenant of love with them. They wept because there was a mutual sincere love evident in their relationship. I cannot help but imagine that Naomi was a mother-in-law who built her relationship with her daughters-in-law on hospitality, grace, and encouragement from the beginning. The destructive behaviors of control and criticism could not have been prominent in this relationship. These young women felt safe with her.

My dear son, may you seek a lovely lady who has a hospitable, gracious, and encouraging disposition. I pray that you will have discernment and wisdom in order to recognize a controlling, critical, and contrite spirit. May your wife provide a safe haven for you and your family. I pray that I do the same no matter what age you are. In a world filled with discouragement, may your wife be a safe place for you to fall. In order for her to be that safe haven, she must not be self-centered. She must seek to serve others, as was the case with both Naomi and Ruth, whose actions were beautiful.

And Naomi said, Turn again, my daughters: why will ye go with me? are there yet any more sons in my womb, that they may be your husbands? Turn again, my daughters, go your way; for I am too old to have an husband. If I should say, I have hope, if I should have an husband also to night, and should also bear sons; Would ye tarry for them till they were grown? would ye stay for them from having husbands? nay, my daughters; for it grieveth me much for your sakes that the hand of the Lord is gone out against me. And they lifted up their voice, and wept again: and Orpah kissed her mother in law; but Ruth clave unto her. And she said, Behold, thy sister in law is gone back unto her people, and unto her gods: return thou after thy sister in law. And Ruth said, Intreat me not to leave thee, or to return from following after thee: for whither thou goest, I will go; and where thou lodgest, I will lodge: thy people shall be my people, and thy God my God: Where thou diest, will I die, and there will I be buried: the Lord do so to me, and more also, if ought but death part thee and me. When she saw that she was stedfastly minded to go with her, then she left speaking unto her. So they two went until they came to Bethlehem. And it came to pass, when they were come to Bethlehem, that all the city was moved about them, and they said, Is this Naomi? And she said unto them, Call me not Naomi, call me Mara: for the Almighty hath dealt very bitterly with me. I went out full and the Lord hath brought me home again empty: why then call ye me Naomi, seeing the Lord hath testified against me, and the Almighty hath afflicted me? So Naomi returned,

and Ruth the Moabitess, her daughter in law, with
her, which returned out of the country of Moab:
and they came to Bethlehem in the beginning of
barley harvest. (Ruth 1:11–22)

Ruth's Loyal Decision

Intreat me not to leave thee, or to return from
following after thee: for whither thou goest, I will
go; and where thou lodgest, I will lodge: thy people
shall be my people, and thy God my God. (Ruth
1:16)

Ruth received the love Naomi gave. She wanted to embrace
Naomi, her people, and the one true God. She was loyal to the
love she had experienced within their family. Even though there
was no assurance in their future, she was sure of the love she had
received from Naomi and her God, and she was sure of the love
she wanted to give in return. These are qualities of a lady of faith.
"Now faith is the substance of things hoped for, the evidence of
things not seen" (Hebrews 11:1). Ruth ultimately believed and had
faith in the fact that as long as she remained loyal to the one true
God, whom she had learned about through her relationship with
Naomi and her family, then everything else would fall into place.
With no assurance of their future, she rested in the assurance of
knowing the One who holds the future in His hands. My dear
son, this is a picture of a godly lady. In life, many times things
will happen that do not make sense, and many situations will
arise that create a need to serve tirelessly without assurance of the
outcome. Because of our faith in the Lord and our trust in Him,
we must keep our mind on the prize set before us. Keeping our
minds on Him and on things eternal is the only way to endure
daily hardships. A lady with this kind of faith will remain true in
sickness and in health, for richer or poorer, until death do you part.

> I went out full and the Lord hath brought me
> home again empty: why then call ye me Naomi,
> seeing the Lord hath testified against me, and the
> Almighty hath afflicted me? So Naomi returned,
> and Ruth the Moabitess, her daughter in law, with
> her, which returned out of the country of Moab:
> and they came to Bethlehem in the beginning of
> barley harvest. (Ruth 1:21–22)

Naomi identified herself as one with whom the Almighty had dealt
bitterly, one who was now empty, and one who had had misfortune
brought against her. There are two truths in these passages. Naomi
acknowledged her sin. She understood that she was suffering the
consequences of her family's sins. This sin was most likely not her
own sin; it was the sin of her husband. The consequences of our
own sin are not felt by us alone. The consequences of sin ripple
throughout the family and those closest to the sinner. This is one
example of the importance of being a husband and father of prayer
and faith, relying on the Lord's provision in your life. *May you be
a husband on whom your wife can safely rely to lead her to safety, not
harm.*

Naomi recognized that by bringing her daughter-in-law, a
Moabitess, and a foreigner back to her land, and if she was to be
able to continue to share the love of the one and only God with
Ruth, that she herself would continue to be identified with the sin
of their family. Naomi also knew that her daughter-in-law might
suffer ridicule. What a picture of faith! Naomi saw a cause greater
than herself. She was willing to be continually identified with
her sin in order to continue to be a good witness to Ruth, placing
Ruth's need above her own. Ruth's desire to continue her walk in
the love of the one true God was important for her growth in her
love and knowledge of the Lord. *Naomi was willing to sacrifice for
the well-being of another.* Truly, this is a beautiful quality of her
heart's desire for others.

The other truth is that Ruth chose to be identified with Naomi. Ruth was willing to serve Naomi though she might be persecuted in this land because she was a foreigner. Ruth was willing to be identified with the afflicted and was willing to endure the misfortunes placed upon them because of her loyalty to the relationship God had brought about between her and Naomi. One who is loyal is one who is willing to serve you no matter how they may appear doing it or how they are looked upon while doing it. It will not matter if they are looked down upon, persecuted, mocked, etc. Jesus was loyal to us all the way to the cross. Ruth was loyal all the way back to the land of Judah, not knowing the outcome of her travels.

Life Application

My dear son, you will make mistakes. Sin will come knocking, and you may choose unwisely in some situations. These sins may not be that serious at times. These "not so serious" types of sin are ones that are easily forgiven and from which those affected are easily able to move on. Sins of this natures include not praying before you buy a car. But some sins are more serious and may cause years of embarrassment and ridicule. Sins like this are so evident to everyone around you that you feel that people no longer look at you the same way. It is a constant reminder of your failure. Sins of this nature include declaring bankruptcy because you did not manage your money well, causing you and your family to lose your home. You want a wife who is willing to serve you even when you have committed a detrimental mistake or made a poor choice or an unwise decision—ultimately, a sin—because she is serving the Lord and is committed to Him. This is a wife of noble character, one who refrains from continuously bringing up past hurts and instead chooses no longer to remember your sins or hold them against you. I am speaking of a lady who is able to move past her hurts and continue to serve the Lord and you in your marriage, one who gets her strength and joy from the Lord, not from man.

Ruth 2

And Naomi had a kinsman of her husband's, a mighty man of wealth, of the family of Elimelech; and his name was Boaz. And Ruth the Moabitess said unto Naomi, Let me now go to the field, and glean ears of corn after him in whose sight I shall find grace. (Ruth 2:1–2)

And he that shall humble himself shall be exalted. (Matthew 23:12)

Ruth said, "Let me now go to the field, and glean ears of corn after him in whose sight I shall find grace." (Ruth 2:2)

Here we see that Ruth not only was loyal but also that she had a servant's heart. She not only saw the need of those in the field but also looked for ways she could meet that need. She did not waste time worrying, planning, or trying to figure out a way for them not to be in need. Instead, she was ready to accept both the responsibility and the burden of assisting them in meeting their needs. She was humble enough not to think of herself as being above the call that had been placed upon her life. This humility is a quality to be desired in a helpmeet. One who displays this magnitude of humility accepts the awesome burden of responsibility in this life. This is a wife who is willing to lay down her desires for her own life in order to meet the needs of her children. She is one who is willing to seek out ways to meet the needs of both you and your loved ones. She is a Ruth. A Ruth does not expect to go out and find favor—she does not think too highly of herself but hopes to "pick up leftovers in whose eyes she finds favor." She is not afraid of the hard work at hand. She accepts the responsibility of this hard work, recognizing that she will not get great rewards but knowingly accepting the hardships of the day in expectation of leftovers—less than the best. A servant's heart indeed is a quality to be desired.

> And she (Naomi) said unto her, Go, my daughter.
> And she went, and came, and gleaned in the field
> after the reapers: and her hap was to light on a part
> of the field belonging unto Boaz, who was of the
> kindred of Elimelech. (Ruth 2:2–3)

The Lord was gracious to Ruth and placed her in the field of Naomi's relative—the one relative available to redeem her and get her out of her situation—but this fact is unbeknownst to her. Sometimes the Lord places us in situations so that we may show ourselves faithful and worthy of His blessings. He places us in situations where we are to prove ourselves willing to serve wholeheartedly without the promise of good, but trusting only in His daily provision. We are to serve because of our love for Him and our love for what is right, not because of what we want or expect in return. Then, when He finds us faithfully serving because of our love for righteousness, He blesses us beyond measure for our faithfulness. He does not always bless us with what we expect, but He blesses us in ways that honor and glorify Him.

> And, behold, Boaz came from Bethlehem, and said
> unto the reapers, The Lord be with you. And they
> answered him, The Lord bless thee. (Ruth 2:4)

Let's look at Boaz. He was the foreman of his harvesters. We see in verse 4 that Boaz went to check on his harvesters, not to see if they were doing their job correctly or if they were doing anything wrong, but to greet them: "The Lord be with you" (Ruth 2:4). This one act tells us so much about his character. He did not come to rule over them, nor did he come to exalt his presence over them so that they would fear reprimand. He came to greet them with a humble attitude—"making himself of no reputation but being equal with them." Their reply, "The Lord bless thee" (Ruth 2:4), is an indication that there was an established mutual respect between this foreman and his workers. They were comfortable enough in his presence to bless him back. Both the master and the servant were showing the love of Christ for one another—theirs is a love that "hopes all things." A love that only comes from Jesus Christ hopes all things, expects good and not harm, and comes in arrival to greet, not to beat; to bless, not to curse; and to honor, not to tear down. An owner who cares enough to speak to his harvesters is one who will take notice of the work that is being done and will also take notice of each worker in his field. Because of his humility of spirit and his pattern of greeting his servants, Boaz knew enough, cared enough, and took enough notice of them that he also noticed that there was a foreign worker in the field. Never underestimate the reward for being thoughtful, respectful, and considerate. Not only do others notice such rare qualities, but also those rare qualities give you an opportunity to be made aware of the needs of those around you. Meeting the needs of others brings a joy to your heart to which nothing else can quite compare.

> Then said Boaz unto his servant that was set over the reapers, Whose damsel is this? And the servant that was set over the reapers answered and said, It is the Moabitish damsel that came back with Naomi out of the country of Moab: And she said, I pray you, let me glean and gather after the reapers among the sheaves: so she came, and hath continued even from the morning until now, that she tarried a little in the house. Then said Boaz unto Ruth, Hearest thou not, my daughter? Go not to glean in another field, neither go from hence, but abide here fast by my maidens: Let thine eyes be on the field that they do reap, and go thou after

them: have I not charged the young men that they shall not touch thee? and when thou art athirst, go unto the vessels, and drink of that which the young men have drawn. (Ruth 2:5–9)

Ruth's Reputation Preceded Her. Reputation Is Important

"Whose damsel is this" (Ruth 2:5)? Ruth's reputation preceded her. The foreman shared with Boaz that Ruth had asked for permission to glean, and that in her request, her humble plea was only for the leftovers, the sheaves left behind. The foreman also described her as one who worked steadily with only a short rest. What a reputation that had already been imparted in such a short statement. This statement not only gives us a picture of Ruth but also shows us how important it is to communicate truth to others in a way that clearly defines the heart and the motive of a person. Selfish people do not want to exalt another for fear that the person they are speaking to will highly favor the one they are speaking of. What if the foreman had said, "That's a woman who came this morning looking for a handout. She stated that she's a poor woman and asked to get our leftovers." If he had not properly communicated the motive of her heart, Boaz would not have seen the beauty in her diligence to work hard for little reward, nor would he have seen the humility in her request. Because he was made aware of her motives, he had compassion toward her and immediately wanted her for his own. "My daughter, Go not to glean in another field … abide here fast by my maidens" (Ruth 2:8). He desired to protect her, telling his men not to touch her. He also wanted to provide for her: "Whenever thou art athirst, go unto the vessels, and drink of that which the young men have drawn" (Ruth 2:9).

This is what Christ is for us. He calls us to Himself. He makes us one of His own children. He protects us under the shelter of His wings. He gives us our daily bread and provides for our every need. He wants us to drink from the water of His well. This is also a picture of how a husband should love and care for his wife. *Nothing makes a lady more secure than knowing that her husband will protect her, provide for her, and care for her every need and the needs of their family.*

> Then she fell on her face, and bowed herself to the ground, and said unto him, Why have I found grace in thine eyes, that thou shouldest take knowledge of me, seeing I am a stranger? (Ruth 2:10)

What a picture of Christ's redeeming grace! Ruth did not respond with, "Finally, I have relief!" or "I knew something would come along!" or "Thank goodness! You saw my need and met it!" No, she responded with the same attitude that a lost person comes to Christ with—"Why would you look upon a sinner such as I and grant me such grace and mercy? I am undeserving." She then bowed her head down toward the ground, recognizing her unworthiness and showing her gratefulness for his redemption.

My son, a lady who has been gloriously saved will forever be humbled by the fact that she was once a sinner and now has been found, that she was not deserving of His grace but is thankful for His redeeming power. She will live with gratitude for every mercy and gift of grace she receives. She will see each day as a gift and make the most of it, recognizing that "this is the day which the Lord hath made; we will rejoice and be glad in it" (Psalm 118:24). Honey, I pray that you will find a wife who is willing to serve with a grateful heart—to serve her Savior, to serve you as a helpmeet, and to serve her family with a meek and quiet spirit, teaching them diligently to love the Lord their God with all their heart, soul, and strength all the days of their lives.

> And Boaz answered and said unto her, It hath fully been shewed me, all that thou hast done unto thy mother in law since the death of thine husband:

and how thou hast left thy father and thy mother,
and the land of thy nativity, and art come unto a
people which thou knewest not heretofore. The
Lord recompense thy work, and a full reward be
given thee of the Lord God of Israel, under whose
wings thou art come to trust. (Ruth 2:11–12)

Boaz recognized Ruth's willingness to meet a need no matter what it
would cost her. "Who can find a virtuous woman" (Proverbs 31:10)?
Virtuous. Boaz found this noble character in Ruth, and it is my
prayer that this is what you will find in a wife, a willingness to meet
the needs of her loved ones no matter the cost. Life is filled with
hardships. It takes a lady of noble character to continue to meet the
needs of her family day in and day out while she faces life's inevitable
hardships. When a person is not grateful when things are going
well, his or her attitude when things go awry becomes worse. Such
a person sees God as being mad at him or her or not being God.

Boaz was able to recognize the noble character of Ruth because
he cared for others enough to make it a practice to check on his
servants' well-being and to bless them. He was concerned enough
about the people around him to reach out, speak, and take notice,
even recognizing that there was an extra worker in the field. He
was willing to take the time to find out more about her and to
concern himself with the details of her needs. Because of his true
interest in the lives of others, he found a lovely lady who was found
to be loyal in every way. My son, you are very interested in people,
and you love to speak to everyone and find out what interests them
in their life. I pray that as you meet new people, you wait patiently
on the Lord to reveal to you without any doubt that you have
found a wife of noble character, one He has set aside just for you.

Boaz was also a man who wanted good, not harm, to come to
Ruth. He was not easily offended. He did not want to get her off
his property. He saw her need and wanted to be a part of the rich
rewards she so deserved.

Then she said, "Let me find favour in thy sight, my lord; for that thou hast comforted me, and for that thou hast spoken friendly unto thine handmaid, though I be not like unto one of thine handmaidens." (Ruth 2:13)

Her response to his kindness was one of humble gratitude. She recognized that he did not have to grant favor—she did not have any sense of entitlement whatsoever. And she was grateful for his favor but did not expect more. She knew to be thankful for today's gift—"Let me find favour in thy sight, my lord" (Ruth 2:13). What a pure response of humble gratitude.

And Boaz said unto her, At mealtime come thou hither, and eat of the bread, and dip thy morsel in the vinegar. And she sat beside the reapers: and he reached her parched corn, and she did eat, and was sufficed, and left. And when she was risen up to glean, Boaz commanded his young men, saying, Let her glean even among the sheaves, and reproach her not: And let fall also some of the handfuls of purpose for her, and leave them, that she may glean them, and rebuke her not. So she gleaned in the field until even, and beat out that she had gleaned: and it was about an ephah of barley. And she took it up, and went into the city: and her mother in law saw what she had gleaned: and she brought forth, and gave to her that she had reserved after she was sufficed. (Ruth 2:14–18)

The fact that Boaz ate with his men reveals even more about his character. He did not see himself as better than they but made himself equal to them. He sat at the table with them, eating together and partaking of the same food. If he had been too proud to have a relationship with these workers, he would have missed out on the wonderful gift of this lovely loyal lady in his midst.

As Christians, we are to strive to be more like Jesus each day in all that we do. In doing so, we follow Jesus's example by making no reputation for ourselves and not thinking of ourselves higher than we ought. We are to be humble. If we glorify ourselves, we'll never serve Him or others in the way we should. Others will never see the love of Christ that we have in our hearts. Because of Boaz's willingness to eat with his workers, which is such a simple gesture, the Lord blessed him with a lady who would be loyal to the Lord and to Boaz all the days of his life. She had also humbled herself to serve another, namely, Naomi. She did not consider herself higher than the calling to serve another.

I believe verse 14b is of great importance: "She had reserved after she was sufficed" (Ruth 2:14b). She was able to have a reserve after she had sufficiently taken some for herself. This is important because it shows that even though her needs were many, she still exhibited self-control. What a beautiful quality in a lady. Son, you want to know that when needs arise, you have a wife who does not have a sense of entitlement; nor does she exhibit behavior that expresses that it is high time she be compensated for her work; nor does she wallow in self-pity, exclaiming that her rude behavior of having eaten it all is excusable because she has gone without. But instead, she remains earnest, humble, and grateful for the gifts given to her. Please note that Ruth's gift was not excessive but was merely bread. A met need is a gift we should not take for granted. If we remain thankful for each daily provision, recognizing that every day is a gift from God, then we will be cautious never to display the rude behavior of selfishness or entitlement, nor will we easily take things or people for granted.

And her mother in law said unto her, Where hast thou gleaned to day? and where wroughtest thou? blessed be he that did take knowledge of thee. And she shewed her mother in law with whom she had wrought, and said, The man's name with whom I wrought to day is Boaz. And Naomi said unto her daughter in law, Blessed be he of the Lord, who hath not left off his kindness to the living and to the dead. And Naomi said unto her, The man is near of kin unto us, one of our next kinsmen. And Ruth the Moabitess said, He said unto me also, Thou shalt keep fast by my young men, until they have ended all my harvest. And Naomi said unto Ruth her daughter in law, It is good, my daughter, that thou go out with his maidens, that they meet thee not in any other field. So she kept fast by the maidens of Boaz to glean unto the end of barley harvest and of wheat harvest; and dwelt with her mother in law. (Ruth 2:19–23)

Boaz, impressed by Ruth's self-control, made sure his workers pulled out some stalks for her. He did not want them to embarrass her in any way, but he made sure that their gift honored her. As you read to the end of this chapter, you will see that even though Boaz saw that Ruth was such a lovely lady, he did not let her know his feelings for her. He let her work the fields throughout the harvest. There is a great lesson to be learned here. Even though you may be impressed by a lady, and even though she may have a lovely heart, loyal through and through, it is important that you observe her in not only triumphs but also trials. Sometimes trials are long. You want someone you can fully trust with your best interests at heart.

Ruth 3

Then Naomi her mother in law said unto her, My daughter, shall I not seek rest for thee, that it may be well with thee? And now is not Boaz of our kindred, with whose maidens thou wast? Behold, he winnoweth barley to night in the threshingfloor. Wash thyself therefore, and anoint thee, and put thy raiment upon thee, and get thee down to the floor: but make not thyself known unto the man, until he shall have done eating and drinking. And it shall be, when he lieth down, that thou shalt mark the place where he shall lie, and thou shalt go in, and uncover his feet, and lay thee down; and he will tell thee what thou shalt do. And she said unto her, All that thou sayest unto me I will do. And she went down unto the floor, and did according to all that her mother in law bade her. And when Boaz had eaten and drunk, and his heart was merry, he went to lie down at the end of the heap of corn: and she came softly, and uncovered his feet, and laid her down. And it came to pass at midnight, that the man was afraid, and turned himself: and, behold, a woman lay at his feet. And he said, Who art thou? And she answered, I am Ruth thine handmaid: spread therefore thy skirt over thine handmaid; for thou art a near kinsman. And he said, Blessed be thou of the Lord, my daughter: for thou hast shewed more kindness in the latter end than at the beginning, inasmuch as thou followedst not young men, whether poor or rich. And now, my daughter, fear not; I will do to thee all that thou requirest: for all the city of my people doth know that thou art a virtuous woman. And now it is true that I am thy near kinsman: howbeit there is a kinsman nearer than I. Tarry this night, and it shall be in the morning, that if he will perform unto thee the part of a kinsman, well; let him do the kinsman's part: but if he will not do the part of a kinsman to thee, then will I do the part of a kinsman to thee, as the Lord liveth: lie down until the morning. And she lay at his feet until the morning: and she rose up before one could know another. And he said, Let it not be known that a woman came into the floor. Also he said, Bring the vail that thou hast upon thee, and hold it. And when she held it, he measured six measures of barley, and laid it on her: and she went into the city. And when she came to her mother in law, she said, Who art thou, my daughter? And she told her all that the man had done to her. And she said, These six measures of barley gave he me; for he said to me, Go not empty unto thy mother in law. Then said she, Sit still, my daughter, until thou know how the matter will fall: for the man will not be in rest, until he have finished the thing this day. (Ruth 3:1–18)

In this chapter, we see the ultimate loyalty and trust of Ruth. She was willing to go to Boaz, risking rejection and ridicule. She was young. I believe she must have been beautiful, yet she was willing to offer herself to Boaz, an older man, because of Naomi's request. Ruth's response to Naomi was, "All that thou sayest unto me I will do" (Ruth 3:5), and she did everything her mother-in-law said to do.

She did not question, she did not complain, and she did not want to desert her service to her mother-in-law. She was still willing to do what needed to be done and to do what was requested of her without wavering. There are times in life, my dear son, when your faith may falter. You may want to give up. Your wife needs to be one who is willing to stay the course, keeping her eyes on the prize—pleasing the Lord should be the ultimate goal. You will want a wife who will be there to encourage you to run the race with perseverance, not one who is looking for a way out. Ruth's willingness to offer herself as a sacrifice is evident. In your pursuit of a wife, look for evidence of the same qualities found in Ruth. Remember, these qualities are character traits that are evident through established behavior. These are not qualities that you can assume will be there or can count on to be there when times are tough. Loyalty, sacrifice, a servant's heart, hard work—these are not qualities that just appear. No, these are qualities that are evident in established relationships. If a woman is not loyal to her family, then she will not be loyal to you. If she is not willing to offer her love sacrificially for her family, then she will not be a sacrificially loving mother. These are not traits that suddenly appear. These are traits within a person's heart that may grow stronger over time, but the traits need to be there in the beginning in order to grow.

My son, what a beautiful truth the book of Ruth reveals to us. Boaz, the kinsman redeemer, was united with a servant whose loyalty and trust was wholly proven to be impeccable. If your marriage is to reflect the qualities that are laid out in the Bible, and if you are to love your wife as God loves the church, then your wife must be one who fully acknowledges Him in all her ways, trusting in Him and leaning not on her own understanding. She must be loyal to the Lord and to her husband, her bridegroom, without wavering. May your marriage be of such a quality that when one of you falls, the other is there to pick you up. May you have an edifying, glorifying, encouraging relationship, one where the two of you spur each other on, where iron sharpens iron. May you recognize each other's weaknesses and be willing to compensate for those weaknesses in each other.

Ruth 4

> Then went Boaz up to the gate, and sat him down
> there: and, behold, the kinsman of whom Boaz

spake came by; unto whom he said, Ho, such a one! turn aside, sit down here. And he turned aside, and sat down. And he took ten men of the elders of the city, and said, Sit ye down here. And they sat down. And he said unto the kinsman, Naomi, that is come again out of the country of Moab, selleth a parcel of land, which was our brother Elimelech's: And I thought to advertise thee, saying, Buy it before the inhabitants, and before the elders of my people. If thou wilt redeem it, redeem it: but if thou wilt not redeem it, then tell me, that I may know: for there is none to redeem it beside thee; and I am after thee. And he said, I will redeem it. Then said Boaz, What day thou buyest the field of the hand of Naomi, thou must buy it also of Ruth the Moabitess, the wife of the dead, to raise up the name of the dead upon his inheritance. And the kinsman said, I cannot redeem it for myself, lest I mar mine own inheritance: redeem thou my right to thyself; for I cannot redeem it. Now this was the manner in former time in Israel concerning redeeming and concerning changing, for to confirm all things; a man plucked off his shoe, and gave it to his neighbour: and this was a testimony in Israel. Therefore the kinsman said unto Boaz, Buy it for thee. So he drew off his shoe. And Boaz said unto the elders, and unto all the people, Ye are witnesses this day, that I have bought all that was Elimelech's, and all that was Chilion's and Mahlon's, of the hand of Naomi. Moreover Ruth the Moabitess, the wife of Mahlon, have I purchased to be my wife, to raise up the name of the dead upon his inheritance, that the name of the dead be not cut off from among his brethren, and from the gate of his place: ye are witnesses this day. And all the people that were in the gate, and the elders, said, We are witnesses. The Lord make the woman that is come into thine house like Rachel and like Leah, which two did build the house of Israel: and do thou worthily in Ephratah, and be famous in Bethlehem: And let thy house be like the house of Pharez, whom Tamar bare unto Judah, of the seed which the Lord shall give thee of this young woman. (Ruth 4:1–12)

This last chapter of the book of Ruth tells a man how he should behave in both his relationships and matters of business. How honorable Boaz was! How trusting he was in God's perfect will being fulfilled! How committed he was to doing what was right no matter how it might impact him and his own personal interests! Do you see it? Do you see the commitment in his actions?

He wanted Ruth for his wife. He loved her. He had already sought to provide for her and to protect her. He had spent time getting to know her. He admired the qualities he had found in her. He wanted her for his bride. But he also knew that according to what was considered right, she was not his to have. He knew he needed to offer his interests to another who was considered the guardian-redeemer. He knew going into this meeting that he needed to bring trusted witnesses with him. The Lord tells us more than once in His Word that we should have witnesses with us in important matters. By doing this, there is no question as to what happened in the meeting, and you may be respected among your elders because you have nothing to hide. Approaching this meeting, Boaz was not trying to find a way to keep Ruth for himself. He was not trying to manipulate the situation for his personal interests. *He honorably accepted the responsibility of doing what was right and was willing to pay the price. This, my son, is a noble quality that is rare and beautiful in a husband.* May you always be willing to strive for righteousness, even in the most difficult of circumstances. After Boaz offered the guardian-redeemer both land and Ruth, the guardian-redeemer graciously denied the offer, allowing Boaz to be the kinsman redeemer. The elders were there to witness the transaction and the communication between the two men. Now Boaz was able to marry Ruth without murmurings or strife. He was blessed not only by her character traits, which he loved in her, but also by his own obedience to the Lord and his strivings to do things in the proper order to find favor with both the Lord and man.

> So Boaz took Ruth, and she was his wife: and when he went in unto her, the Lord gave her conception, and she bare a son. And the women said unto Naomi, Blessed be the Lord, which hath not left thee this day without a kinsman, that his name may be famous in Israel. And he shall be unto thee a restorer of thy life, and a nourisher of thine old age: for thy daughter in law, which loveth thee, which is better to thee than seven sons, hath born him. And Naomi took the child, and laid it in her bosom, and became nurse unto it. And the women her neighbours gave it a name, saying, There is a son born to Naomi; and they called his name Obed: he is the father of Jesse, the father of David. (Ruth 4:13–17)

The Lord's grace and mercy is abundant. He had given Boaz and Ruth a son. The Lord granted them a new life. The old was gone, and the new had begun. Sin had a detrimental consequence for Naomi, but forgiveness brought about new beginnings. Sin had caused pain for Ruth, but her commitment to serving Him was blessed by God. Boaz's commitment to righteousness, his willingness to lose what he loved for a greater cause, allowed him to experience abundant grace. He became not only the husband to a virtuous woman but also the great-grandfather to King David. Praise the Lord for giving us such a wonderful picture of the Lord's faithfulness to us when we are committed to Him (i.e., Boaz). Praise the Lord for giving us such a wonderful picture of His faithfulness to us when we have strayed and then we rededicate our lives to Him (i.e., Naomi). Praise the Lord for giving us such a wonderful picture of His faithfulness to us when we recognize His almighty hand and are willing to work tirelessly for Him because we have experienced His love in our lives, even though we may have suffered because of someone else's sin (i.e., Ruth). We love Him because He first loved us.

Dear Lord,

May my dear son be a man like Boaz, humble, willing to wait, and willing to do what is right even when he stands to lose all that is dear to him. May he find a wife who recognizes the love of the Savior. May she be one who is willing to cheerfully work hard at all she does because she is working for You, Lord. May their relationship be one that You will bless abundantly with Your grace and mercy. May he and his wife see every day as a gift. May their hearts be filled with gratitude. May they live for You, love You, and serve You throughout their lives. May they teach their children to love You, Lord, as their God with all their hearts, all their strength, and all their might.

In Jesus's name, I pray. Amen.

CHAPTER 2

Isaac and Rebekah

Genesis 24

And Abraham was old, and well stricken in age: and the Lord had blessed Abraham in all things. And Abraham said unto his eldest servant of his house, that ruled over all that he had, Put, I pray thee, thy hand under my thigh: And I will make thee swear by the Lord, the God of heaven, and the God of the earth, that thou shalt not take a wife unto my son of the daughters of the Canaanites, among whom I dwell: But thou shalt go unto my country, and to my kindred, and take a wife unto my son Isaac. (Genesis 24:1–4)

My Son,

No matter how old one is and no matter the time period, *a parent wants what is best for his or her child. The thought of the child entangling himself with the enemy is unbearable.* Abraham wanted a wife who had the same beliefs as his family, a wife who would instill the same values of the Lord in their offspring.

> And the servant said unto him, Peradventure the woman will not be willing to follow me unto this land: must I needs bring thy son again unto the land from whence thou camest? And Abraham said unto him, Beware thou that thou bring not my son thither again. The Lord God of heaven, which took me from my father's house, and from the land of my kindred, and which spake unto me, and that sware unto me, saying, Unto thy seed will I give this land; he shall send his angel before thee, and thou shalt take a wife unto my son from thence. And if the woman will not be willing to follow thee, then thou shalt be clear from this my oath: only bring not my son thither again. And the servant put his hand under the thigh of Abraham his master, and sware to him concerning that matter. (Genesis 24:5–9)

The difference between Elimilech, Ruth's father-in-law, and Abraham is that Abraham was not willing to let his son have the opportunity to fall in love with the enemy and learn the enemy's ways. Even though Isaac was grown, Abraham continued until his death to protect Isaac. Abraham instilled two disciplines: to flee from evil and to abstain from all appearances of evil. Abraham knew what the Lord had told him. He clung to the promise even on his deathbed. His faith did not waver, nor did he compromise. He knew that the Lord would bless Isaac with offspring and that there was a great inheritance in store for their family. He took action to ensure that Isaac had a wife who loved the Lord her God with all her heart.

> And the servant took ten camels of the camels of his master, and departed; for all the goods of his master were in his hand: and he arose, and went to Mesopotamia, unto the city of Nahor. And he made his camels to kneel down without the city by a well of water at the time of the evening, even the time that women go out to draw water. And he said O Lord God of my master Abraham, I pray thee, send me good speed this day, and shew kindness unto my master Abraham. Behold, I stand here by the well of water; and the daughters of the men of the city come out to draw water: And let it come to pass, that the damsel to whom I shall say, Let down thy pitcher, I pray thee, that I may drink; and she shall say, Drink, and I will give thy camels drink also: let the same be she that thou hast appointed for thy servant Isaac; and thereby shall I know that thou hast shewed kindness unto my master. (Genesis 24:10–14)

Son, I want you to look closely at this servant for a moment. The servant's name is *never* mentioned. His business was to act in accordance with Abraham's will. This servant *never* spoke of himself, nor did he promote himself. This servant had to travel five hundred miles on foot with ten camels to find his master a suitable bride for his son. This journey was so important that it was *not* thought to have been too much for the task. Our job as servants should be something that we see as most important until the very last task is complete. The job of a servant never ends.[3]

---

[3] Greg Butler, pastor of Bible Baptist Church of Monroe, ww.biblebapt.org.

Things to learn from the servant are as follows:

1. Seek not to exalt yourself.

   No matter how hard the task, no matter how mundane the job, no matter how tired you are, and no matter how senseless what you're doing seems, remember whom you are serving. "And whatsoever ye do, do it heartily, as to the Lord, and not unto men" (Colossians 3:23).

2. Don't make excuses or justifications for why you should not complete the task you have been given. Do it without complaint.

3. Be mindful of your audience, which is an audience of one.

4. Trust and obey.

5. Pray for a tangible confirmation. Be as specific as Abraham was in his prayer. Ask, "If she is the one, Lord, please show me by having her respond to my request with a servant's heart."

6. Be willing to do hard things. Go to her family. Share with them the purpose of your pursuit. Share with them the traits that the Lord has shown you through her behavior, and how He has confirmed to you that you should pursue her and get to know her better.

May your family be blessed by the addition of her presence. May your family have peace in knowing that you have prayed and received confirmation to pursue this lady to take as your wife. May you have a standard that she must meet before you even consider her as a possible helpmeet. May you choose wisely someone who has the same beliefs as you. May she be one who loves the Lord with all her heart, mind, soul, and strength. May she be one whom you and your family can trust to train your children to love and serve the Lord.

And it came to pass, before he had done speaking, that, behold, Rebekah came out, who was born to Bethuel, son of Milcah, the wife of Nahor, Abraham's brother, with her pitcher upon her shoulder. And the damsel was very fair to look upon, a virgin, neither had any man known her: and she went down to the well, and filled her pitcher, and came up. And the servant ran to meet her, and said, Let me, I pray thee, drink a little water of thy pitcher. And she said, Drink, my lord: and she hasted, and let down her pitcher upon her hand, and gave him drink. And when she had done giving him drink, she said, I will draw water for thy camels also, until they have done drinking. And she hasted, and emptied her pitcher into the trough, and ran again unto the well to draw water, and drew for all his camels. And the man wondering at her held his peace, to wit whether the Lord had made his journey prosperous or not. (Genesis 24:15–21)

The Lord graciously answered the servant's plea, yet the servant remained prudent. *He did not immediately assume, because she'd said the right words in response to his request, that she was the one the Lord had for Isaac. No, he continued to watch and observe.*

Do you know that camels drink five gallons of water at a time? Camels drink five gallons of water at a time! This servant had ten camels![4] When he asked the Lord to show him the lady he had set out for Isaac, he was very specific. She watered those camels until they had their fill while the servant watched. What do you think he saw? What would further confirm to him that she was the one the Lord had set apart for Isaac?

She displayed meekness. She was willing to serve without resentment.

---

[4] Ibid.

She was a lady of character. She did what she'd offered to do and completed the task.

She was a hard worker. She did not complain. She did not skimp. She worked hard until the job was done, all while he sat and watched. Now that is a lady with a servant's heart!

She was both caring and compassionate. She saw his needs. She knew he was tired. She saw not only his needs but also the needs of those in his care.

She was a safe haven! If she was willing to do all of this for a stranger, then how much more would she be willing to do for her husband and children one day?

The servant had received confirmation from the Lord that this was the lady set aside for Isaac. The servant's role teaches us never to give up on doing good! This was a five-hundred-mile journey! The first miles and the last miles can sometimes seem like the hardest to complete,[5] but the miles in the middle are the redundant miles that seem never to end. The reward for not giving up is such a blessing! His Word tells us that we will reap a harvest! It is worth it! Wait patiently for the Lord, and keep on keeping on. Trust and obey.

> And it came to pass, as the camels had done drinking, that the man took a golden earring of half a shekel weight, and two bracelets for her hands of ten shekels weight of gold; And said, Whose daughter art thou? tell me, I pray thee: is there room in thy father's house for us to lodge in? And she said unto him, I am the daughter of Bethuel the son of Milcah, which she bare unto Nahor. She said moreover unto him, We have both straw and provender enough, and room to lodge in. And the man bowed down his head, and

---

[5] Ibid.

worshipped the Lord. And he said, Blessed be the
Lord God of my master Abraham, who hath not
left destitute my master of his mercy and his truth:
I being in the way, the Lord led me to the house of
my master's brethren. (Genesis 24:22–27)

The servant never took credit for what had been accomplished that
day. He praised the Lord. He worshipped Him. He was thankful.
Even in his thankfulness, it was not all about what the Lord had
done for him, but about his thankfulness for how the Lord had
blessed his master. Then he praised the Lord for leading him.
What a testimony of humility!

And the damsel ran, and told them of her mother's
house these things. And Rebekah had a brother,
and his name was Laban: and Laban ran out unto
the man, unto the well. And it came to pass, when
he saw the earring and bracelets upon his sister's
hands, and when he heard the words of Rebekah
his sister, saying, Thus spake the man unto me;
that he came unto the man; and, behold, he stood
by the camels at the well. And he said, Come in,
thou blessed of the Lord; wherefore standest thou
without? for I have prepared the house, and room
for the camels. And the man came into the house:
and he ungirded his camels, and gave straw and
provender for the camels, and water to wash his
feet, and the men's feet that were with him. And
there was set meat before him to eat: but he said,
I will not eat, until I have told mine errand. And
he said, Speak on. And he said, I am Abraham's
servant. And the Lord hath blessed my master
greatly; and he is become great: and he hath given
him flocks, and herds, and silver, and gold, and

menservants, and maidservants, and camels, and asses. And Sarah my master's wife bare a son to my master when she was old: and unto him hath he given all that he hath. And my master made me swear, saying, Thou shalt not take a wife to my son of the daughters of the Canaanites, in whose land I dwell: But thou shalt go unto my father's house, and to my kindred, and take a wife unto my son. And I said unto my master, Peradventure the woman will not follow me. And he said unto me, The Lord, before whom I walk, will send his angel with thee, and prosper thy way; and thou shalt take a wife for my son of my kindred, and of my father's house: Then shalt thou be clear from this my oath, when thou comest to my kindred; and if they give not thee one, thou shalt be clear from my oath. And I came this day unto the well, and said, O Lord God of my master Abraham, if now thou do prosper my way which I go: Behold, I stand by the well of water; and it shall come to pass, that when the virgin cometh forth to draw water, and I say to her, Give me, I pray thee, a little water of thy pitcher to drink; And she say to me, Both drink thou, and I will also draw for thy camels: let the same be the woman whom the Lord hath appointed out for my master's son. And before I had done speaking in mine heart, behold, Rebekah came forth with her pitcher on her shoulder; and she went down unto the well, and drew water: and I said unto her, Let me drink, I pray thee. And she made haste, and let down her pitcher from her shoulder, and said, Drink, and I will give thy camels drink also: so I drank, and she made the camels drink also. (Genesis 24:28–46)

Do you see how attentive to detail this servant was? Do you see how he communicated *exactly* what transpired that led him to their daughter/sister? There is much to learn from this servant. He did not say, "The Lord has shown me that your daughter is to be my master's son's wife. I received confirmation from the Lord." He did not expect her family to trust him, nor did he expect them not to question him. No, he cared enough about his master's business to explain in detail why he was sent, where he was sent, and how the Lord orchestrated his encounter with Rebekah. He cared enough about her family to give them the exact details of how the Lord led him to Rebekah. He respected their love for her and their need for answers just as much as he respected the task that he had been given. *This servant is considerate and patient.* In your service to anyone, my dear son, *whether it be your service to your family or your service to others, practice the golden rule, doing unto others as you would have them do unto you.*

> And now if ye will deal kindly and truly with my master, tell me: and if not, tell me; that I may turn to the right hand, or to the left. Then Laban and Bethuel answered and said, The thing proceedeth from the Lord: we cannot speak unto thee bad or good. Behold, Rebekah is before thee, take her, and go, and let her be thy master's son's wife, as the Lord hath spoken. And it came to pass, that, when Abraham's servant heard their words, he worshipped the Lord, bowing himself to the earth. And the servant brought forth jewels of silver, and jewels of gold, and raiment, and gave them to Rebekah: he gave also to her brother and to her mother precious things. And they did eat and drink, he and the men that were with him, and tarried all night; and they rose up in the morning, and he said, Send me away unto my master. And

her brother and her mother said, Let the damsel abide with us a few days, at the least ten; after that she shall go. And he said unto them, Hinder me not, seeing the Lord hath prospered my way; send me away that I may go to my master. And they said, We will call the damsel, and enquire at her mouth. And they called Rebekah, and said unto her, Wilt thou go with this man? And she said, I will go. (Genesis 24:49–58)

Rebekah was a lady of impeccable character. She demonstrated kindness and initiative. She was selfless. She was willing to go. She was willing to stay. Whatever it took, she was willing.

And they sent away Rebekah their sister, and her nurse, and Abraham's servant, and his men. And they blessed Rebekah, and said unto her, Thou art our sister, be thou the mother of thousands of millions, and let thy seed possess the gate of those which hate them. And Rebekah arose, and her damsels, and they rode upon the camels, and followed the man: and the servant took Rebekah, and went his way. And Isaac came from the way of the well Lahairoi; for he dwelt in the south country. And Isaac went out to meditate in the field at the eventide: and he lifted up his eyes, and saw, and, behold, the camels were coming. And Rebekah lifted up her eyes, and when she saw Isaac, she lighted off the camel. For she had said unto the servant, What man is this that walketh in the field to meet us? And the servant had said, It is my master: therefore she took a vail, and covered herself. (Genesis 24:59–65)

What a wonderful young lady of character she was! Upon the sight of her future husband, she pulled her veil over her face in reverence and respect for him and as a sign of purity.

> "And the servant told Isaac all things that he had done" (Genesis 24:66).

Genesis 25

> And these are the generations of Isaac, Abraham's son: Abraham begat Isaac: And Isaac was forty years old when he took Rebekah to wife, the daughter of Bethuel the Syrian of Padanaram, the sister to Laban the Syrian. And Isaac intreated the Lord for his wife, because she was barren: and the Lord was intreated of him, and Rebekah his wife conceived. (Genesis 25:19–21)

> Isaac was threescore years old when she bare them. (Genesis 25:26b)

A husband must be active on his wife's behalf. Not only does God call you to be the provider and protector, but also you need to be your wife's intercessor in prayer. "Isaac intreated the Lord for his wife, because she was barren" (Genesis 25:21). Verse 26 of this scriptures lets us know that he prayed around twenty years for his wife, as he was sixty when she finally gave birth.[6] May your faith be earnest and steadfast like Isaac's.

> And the children struggled together within her; and she said, If it be so, why am I thus? And she went to enquire of the Lord. And the Lord said

---

[6] Ibid.

unto her, Two nations are in thy womb, and two manner of people shall be separated from thy bowels; and the one people shall be stronger than the other people; and the elder shall serve the younger. And when her days to be delivered were fulfilled, behold, there were twins in her womb. And the first came out red, all over like an hairy garment; and they called his name Esau. And after that came his brother out, and his hand took hold on Esau's heel; and his name was called Jacob: and Isaac was threescore years old when she bare them. And the boys grew: and Esau was a cunning hunter, a man of the field; and Jacob was a plain man, dwelling in tents. And Isaac loved Esau, because he did eat of his venison: but Rebekah loved Jacob. (Genesis 25:22–28)

Even though Isaac loved the Lord and had a wife who served and submitted, he allowed there to be unjust favor in his home, and thus jealousy ensued. He was a usable vessel to stir up dissension between the two boys. He set the perfect stage for two nations to be against each other. This was the Lord's plan, and Isaac was the perfect imperfect leader of his household to accomplish this plan of division. My son, please make sure the appetite you create in your home and in your children is an appetite for peace, love, and harmony, not dissension, jealousy, and hatred. May you be a usable vessel for His glory, not a usable vessel for division.

Isaac and Rebekah were of the same people. They were appointed for one another, yet when they became parents, they each took a favorite child. Favoritism is not of God. *The Lord wants you to be disciplined enough to love every child you are given with an unselfish, sacrificial love because every child is a gift from God.* Yes, it is easier to love those who are like-minded with you. "For if ye love them which love you, what reward have ye? do not even the publicans the same? And if ye salute your brethren only, what do ye more than others? do not even the publicans so" (Matthew 5:46–47)? Even pagans love those who treat them well. You must be willing to see what the Lord has given each child in each child's heart. Each one is made in His image with a gift and a purpose. Find their strengths. Love how God made them unique. Seek out the purposes for each child entrusted to your care. Misguided favor leads to resentment. Resentment easily leads to dishonest means.

> And Jacob sod pottage: and Esau came from the field, and he was faint: And Esau said to Jacob, Feed me, I pray thee, with that same red pottage; for I am faint: therefore was his name called Edom. And Jacob said, Sell me this day thy birthright. And Esau said, Behold, I am at the point to die: and what profit shall this birthright do to me? And Jacob said, Swear to me this day; and he sware unto him: and he sold his birthright unto Jacob. Then Jacob gave Esau bread and pottage of lentiles; and he did eat and drink, and rose up, and went his way: thus Esau despised his birthright. (Genesis 25:29–34)

Genesis 26

> And there was a famine in the land, beside the first famine that was in the days of Abraham. And Isaac went unto Abimelech king of the Philistines unto Gerar. And the Lord appeared unto him, and said, Go not down into Egypt; dwell in the land which I shall tell thee of: Sojourn in this land, and I will be with thee, and will bless thee; for unto thee, and unto thy seed, I will give all these countries, and I will perform the oath which I

sware unto Abraham thy father; And I will make thy seed to multiply as the stars of heaven, and will give unto thy seed all these countries; and in thy seed shall all the nations of the earth be blessed; Because that Abraham obeyed my voice, and kept my charge, my commandments, my statutes, and my laws. And Isaac dwelt in Gerar: And the men of the place asked him of his wife; and he said, "She is my sister: for he feared to say, She is my wife; lest, said he, the men of the place should kill me for Rebekah; because she was fair to look upon. And it came to pass, when he had been there a long time, that Abimelech king of the Philistines looked out at a window, and saw, and, behold, Isaac was sporting with Rebekah his wife. And Abimelech called Isaac, and said, Behold, of a surety she is thy wife; and how saidst thou, "She is my sister? And Isaac said unto him, Because I said, Lest I die for her." (Genesis 26:1–9)

Isaac had a godly father who trusted the Lord and picked up his belongings and allowed himself to be led by the Lord alone. Even though Isaac's father, Abraham, trusted the Lord and followed His leading in his life, he too lied to others about his wife, Sarah, telling them that she was his sister, not his wife. Again, this is a perfect example of the father's sin falling onto the son. *But every man must decide for himself from whom he gains his strength. The chains or heritage of sin can be broken. As your daddy and I have said throughout your life, "We're breaking the chains!"*

Isaac chose not to be honest about Rebekah being his wife. He ultimately displayed his doubt in the Lord's sovereignty and in His ability to protect his family by choosing to deceive the men into thinking Rebekah was his sister instead of his wife. This small act of worldly intelligence to protect his family had profound consequences. Never underestimate the power of your witness in seemingly harmless acts and small deceptions (little white lies). Lies that you reason are acceptable because of your circumstances have tremendous consequences. Especially as a husband, a father, and the leader of your household, you set the example of how to conduct oneself. How you behave will one day be displayed in the behavior of your children. Isaac's deception ultimately was used against him as he was dying.

Genesis 27

And it came to pass, that when Isaac was old, and his eyes were dim, so that he could not see, he called Esau his eldest son, and said unto him, My son: and he said unto him, Behold, here am I. And he said, Behold now, I am old, I know not the day of my death: Now therefore take, I pray thee, thy weapons, thy quiver and thy bow, and go out to the field, and take me some venison; And make me savoury meat, such as I love, and bring it to me, that I may eat; that my soul may bless thee before I die. And Rebekah heard when Isaac spake to Esau his son. And Esau went to the field to hunt for venison, and to bring it. And Rebekah spake unto Jacob her son, saying, Behold, I heard thy father speak unto Esau thy brother, saying, Bring me venison, and make me savoury meat, that I may eat, and bless thee before the Lord before my death. Now therefore, my son, obey my voice according to that which I command thee. Go now to the flock, and fetch me from thence two good kids of the goats; and I will make them savoury meat for thy father, such as he loveth: And thou shalt bring it to thy father, that he may eat,

and that he may bless thee before his death. And
Jacob said to Rebekah his mother, Behold, Esau my
brother is a hairy man, and I am a smooth man:
My father peradventure will feel me, and I shall
seem to him as a deceiver; and I shall bring a curse
upon me, and not a blessing. And his mother said
unto him, "Upon me be thy curse, my son: only
obey my voice, and go fetch me them." (Genesis
27:1–13)

What happened to Rebekah?

How did she go from being a young lady of character, whose
character was evident in all she did, who upon the sight of her
future husband pulled her veil over her face in reverence and
respect for him and as a sign of purity, to a lady who at the later
stages of her life was known for deceiving her husband and
encouraging her son to deceive his father while the latter was on
his deathbed?

What happened between, "Drink my lord … I will draw water
for thy camels also" (Genesis 24:18) and "She said to Jacob, 'Look, I
overheard your father say to your brother Esau to get some food so
that he may give him the blessing. … Let the curse fall on me …
only obey my voice'" (Genesis 27:6–13)? In other words, she was
saying, "Do what I say!"

I believe there is so much to be learned from this account of
Isaac and Rebekah's life:

1. We see that Isaac and Rebekah shared favoritism throughout
    the years when they reared their sons. Isaac favored Esau,
    while Rebekah favored Jacob. Isaac did not confront the
    sin of favoritism for whatever reason. Maybe he was too
    busy providing or serving to notice, only noticing when it
    was too late. No matter the reason, the damage was already

done. The evidence of discontentment and greed was shown within the hearts of his sons. Rebekah may have grown weary with Isaac and his nonconfrontational attitude toward this sin. Or maybe she felt he wasn't there, not involved. Maybe she did go to him and he didn't act. Maybe she didn't. Maybe she stayed in her bitter, critical attitude, waiting for him to take a stand. We don't know. Maybe over the years, she had lost some respect for his leadership of the family, causing her to have an idea: *I can do it on my own. I'm home with these boys all day long. I know what's best for them.*

2. *Beware, my son; your responsibility as a husband never ends. It is a daily discipline to continue to love and nurture the relationships you have with your wife and children.* As the years progress and routines are established, it can become very easy to take your loved ones for granted. You must remain diligent in leading them, listening to them, and addressing issues as they occur. When a man is blessed with a wife who takes great care of his children and his home, it is easy for him to believe the lie that his only job is to provide. No, you must remain proactive in your leadership of your family.

3. For whatever reason, in these last days of Isaac's life, he found himself with his "fixer" wife rearing her ugly head.

   She told Jacob that she *overheard* his father. No, the scripture says that Rebekah was listening. Wives tend to do that when they don't have confidence in their husband's leadership. They will listen to "make sure" their husband says the right thing, make sure they say it correctly, etc.

   She was listening to what Isaac was telling Esau. She did not agree with what he had decided to do. She then determined a course of action that would give her the results that she deemed as best for her and her son, but her manipulative deception wreaked havoc on her family in ways that she had not anticipated.

Again I ask, what happened to Rebekah?

Rebekah was a young lady of impeccable character, but she grew into a deceptive wife.

We will never know how or exactly why her character transformed so drastically, but we need to heed the warning in this account of her relationship with Isaac. If she had the ability to change this drastically over the course of time, then we have the potential to change this drastically too. This ability to change should serve as a warning to us all to always guard our hearts. The practice of guarding our hearts should be a daily discipline. None of us are immune to the hardening of the heart.

What is the lesson to be learned through Rebekah's role as a wife?

Lesson 1

We could blame Isaac for not leading and for showing favoritism, but we all know that in many families the wife sets the tone. If Rebekah had come to him early on when she first saw favoritism and gently shared with him how she could see its ugly effects on their sons, he may have turned from that pattern of sin. *Make sure always to be open to your wife's concerns for your family. Don't discount her concern or her desire for your family. Be willing to work on things together. Be a team together.* Be someone with whom she can share her heart and on whom she can rely to do your best to help achieve the goals for your family that you and she set together. Be willing to address sin.

Lesson 2

Maybe in her heart Rebekah liked having one son to call her own; she liked having her child be so very close to her. She may have enjoyed her one child who wanted to be with her the most.

Maybe it fulfilled a selfish desire in her heart. We just don't know the cause, but we are definitely able to see that neither her sin nor her husband's sin was addressed. This pattern led to a change of heart that brought deception and distrust into their family.

My son, you are to lead. Be willing to address areas in your wife's role as both wife and mother that concern you. *You must be willing to make your standards of behavior known from the beginning of your relationship and be willing to address them when there is an issue. It may be hard, but it is your duty as the leader of your family. You wife will respect you for it.*

Lesson 3

This family in scripture should serve to warn us all that we can just as easily fall into this trap of sin. This couple came from godly families. They had a great heritage of faith. They heeded their parents' leadership in their lives. Isaac prayed for twenty years for children.

We have all seen relationships that begin with adoration and then fall into disgust. Be on your guard. Remain respectful. Be respectable. Be loving and considerate.

We have all been in relationships where it is hard to express our concerns. We must express our concerns anyway. When a need arises, my son, if you will remember to place your trust in the Lord in all things, He will be your Rock. Come to the Lord. Tell Him your concerns about your relationship. Ask Him also to reveal these concerns to your spouse. Pray to the Lord to allow you the opportunity to share your heart with your spouse, and ask Him to prepare her heart to receive what He has laid on your heart to share. When you do speak with your spouse, always begin the conversation with a prayer together. Ask the Lord to bless your conversation. Pray, "Let the words of my mouth, and the meditation of my heart, be acceptable in thy sight, O Lord, my strength, and my Redeemer" (Psalm 19:14). Then, trust in the Lord to guide your conversation and confidently address your concerns.

Lesson 4

Considering the great men of faith, what character qualities did they display? What character qualities did their wives display?

Noah was a *righteous man with a sincere faith*. Mrs. Noah must have been a *supportive wife* as there is no record of her questioning him, complaining to him, or doubting him. She followed him into the ark even though she hadn't seen a drop of rain. We do not see a woman who is ashamed of her husband's foolish behavior. No, we see *a submitted wife who trusted that her husband was following the Lord's leadership in his life.*

Abraham moved around and lived in tents. When the Lord asked him to move, he moved. *He was obedient.* His wife was willing to go wherever he went. She did not look at everyone else's house and say, "Why can't we be like that family over there. Everyone else is living this way. Why can't we have a home like that?" Abraham must have established a loving style of leadership in his home. He must have chosen a wife who loved him for who he was and not for what he could give her. *She was willing to go wherever he went.*

Moses stood up for what was right no matter what it cost him. He was willing to live with the slaves and would have rather lived right than live in a palace and be wrong. He was a man of *integrity*. Mrs. Moses did not grumble that they could have been living in a palace and have prominence if only he would have just stayed in the good graces of the king. No, she had the *utmost respect* for her husband and was *content* under his leadership.

Joshua was *faithful* even when what was requested of him did not make sense. Mrs. Joshua was *not critical*. She did not say, "Are you sure that's what you're supposed to do, march around for seven days blowing trumpets?"

And he went, and fetched, and brought them to his mother: and his mother made savoury meat, such as his father loved. And Rebekah took goodly raiment of her eldest son Esau, which were with her in the house, and put them upon Jacob her younger son: And she put the skins of the kids of the goats upon his hands, and upon the smooth of his neck: And she gave the savoury meat and the bread, which she had prepared, into the hand of her son Jacob. And he came unto his father, and said, My father: and he said, Here am I; who art thou, my son? And Jacob said unto his father, I am Esau thy first born; I have done according as thou badest me: arise, I pray thee, sit and eat of my venison, that thy soul may bless me. And Isaac said unto his son, How is it that thou hast found it so quickly, my son? And he said, Because the Lord thy God brought it to me. And Isaac said unto Jacob, Come near, I pray thee, that I may feel thee, my son, whether thou be my very son Esau or not. And Jacob went near unto Isaac his father; and he felt him, and said, The voice is Jacob's voice, but the hands are the hands of Esau. And he discerned him not, because his hands were hairy, as his brother Esau's hands: so he blessed him. And he said, Art thou my very son Esau? And he said, I am. And he said, Bring it near to me, and I will eat of my son's venison, that my soul may bless thee. And he brought it near to him, and he did eat: and he brought him wine and he drank. And his father Isaac said unto him, Come near now, and kiss me, my son. And he came near, and kissed him: and he smelled the smell of his raiment, and blessed him, and said, See, the smell of my son is

47

as the smell of a field which the Lord hath blessed: Therefore God give thee of the dew of heaven, and the fatness of the earth, and plenty of corn and wine: Let people serve thee, and nations bow down to thee: be lord over thy brethren, and let thy mother's sons bow down to thee: cursed be every one that curseth thee, and blessed be he that blesseth thee. And it came to pass, as soon as Isaac had made an end of blessing Jacob, and Jacob was yet scarce gone out from the presence of Isaac his father, that Esau his brother came in from his hunting. And he also had made savoury meat, and brought it unto his father, and said unto his father, Let my father arise, and eat of his son's venison, that thy soul may bless me. And Isaac his father said unto him, Who art thou? And he said, I am thy son, thy firstborn Esau. And Isaac trembled very exceedingly, and said, Who? where is he that hath taken venison, and brought it me, and I have eaten of all before thou camest, and have blessed him? yea, and he shall be blessed. And when Esau heard the words of his father, he cried with a great and exceeding bitter cry, and said unto his father, Bless me, even me also, O my father. And he said, Thy brother came with subtilty, and hath taken away thy blessing. And he said, Is not he rightly named Jacob? for he hath supplanted me these two times: he took away my birthright; and, behold, now he hath taken away my blessing. And he said, Hast thou not reserved a blessing for me? And Isaac answered and said unto Esau, Behold, I have made him thy lord, and all his brethren have I given to him for servants; and with corn and wine have I sustained him: and what shall I do now unto thee, my son? And Esau said unto his father, Hast thou but one blessing, my father? bless me, even me also, O my father. And Esau lifted up his voice, and wept. And Isaac his father answered and said unto him, Behold, thy dwelling shall be the fatness of the earth, and of the dew of heaven from above; And by thy sword shalt thou live, and shalt serve thy brother; and it shall come to pass when thou shalt have the dominion, that thou shalt break his yoke from off thy neck. And Esau hated Jacob because of the blessing wherewith his father blessed him: and Esau said in his heart, The days of mourning for my father are at hand; then will I slay my brother Jacob. And these words of Esau her elder son were told to Rebekah: and she sent and called Jacob her younger son, and said unto him, Behold, thy brother Esau, as touching thee, doth comfort himself, purposing to kill thee. Now therefore, my son, obey my voice; arise, flee thou to Laban my brother to Haran; And tarry with him a few days, until thy brother's fury turn away; Until thy brother's anger turn away from thee, and he forget that which thou hast done to him: then I will send, and fetch thee from thence: why should I be deprived also of you both in one day? And Rebekah said to Isaac, I am weary of my life because of the daughters of Heth: if Jacob take a wife of the daughters of Heth, such as these which are of the daughters of the land, what good shall my life do me? (Genesis 27:14–46)

So, at the end of Isaac's life, the same worldly intelligence was used on him that we saw Isaac display when he denied the fact that Rebekah was, indeed, his wife. This so-called worldly intelligence was an act of deception that he used to protect his own interests. Rebekah, whom he had allowed to favor one son over another, conjured up a way for her favorite son to have the birthright. She relied on deception—the same deception she had seen her husband use to protect his interests. She led Isaac to believe that Jacob was Esau, so he gave his blessing to him. You see, my son, in the end your sin will come back to you. Sometimes your sin will be found out immediately; sometimes it won't. I consider it a blessing if it is found out immediately because then there is usually an immediate consequence. It is exposed. Hopefully you learn from it and then move on, striving for righteousness with a repentant heart. But when a sin continues to linger as a pattern of behavior, the consequences accrue. In order for sin to linger, you must ignore the evidence of its implications on you and those around you. In this ignorance, you are giving an opportunity for those sins to grow into more sin.

A Deeper Look at Genesis 27:21

> And Isaac said unto Jacob, Come near, I pray thee,
> that I may feel thee, my son, whether thou be my
> very son Esau or not. (Genesis 27:21)

This is one of the saddest verses in the account of Isaac. Here he is on his deathbed, and he cannot trust that someone in his household is not deceiving him. My son, you must strive to live a life of flawless character. Your family will learn your ways and will follow that path. I pray that you prayerfully seek your wife, trusting in the Lord to provide her for you. May you learn of her ways, learn of her love for her Lord, and learn of her love for her family. I also implore you to be a leader in your home, one who expects honesty, truth, and sacrificial love. These are not demands made, but these are patterns set by integrity that is established through a saving relationship with our Lord Jesus Christ. As a husband, you lead by example in a loving, honest, trustworthy, and sincere relationship that honors the Lord. You are to serve your family. With this kind of leadership, you should be able to safely trust in your relationship with your wife and have full confidence that she will not only love the Lord with all her heart but will also love you with all her heart, and that she will raise your children to serve and honor the Lord with all their hearts and will teach them right from wrong. Through this mutual love for the Lord and one another, you will be able to share with her, knowing that she is trustworthy, sincere in her faith, and capable as a helpmeet and in motherhood. There is nothing sweeter than the love that God pours into our hearts through His Spirit. His love gives you the ability to "beareth all things, believeth all things, hopeth all things, and endureth all things" (1 Corinthians 13:5–7).

Rebekah was a fixer. Instead of trusting in her husband's position of authority placed over their household by God, she wanted to "fix" the pouring out of blessings to Jacob's advantage. She is an example of one who is not willing to submit to what she perceives to be difficult circumstances. True submission is yielding to the authority placed in your life by God, no matter if it makes sense or not, because in doing so you are ultimately submitting to the authority of God. He has placed this authority there. He knows the decisions that this authority is making. Ultimately, true submission is true submission to God's sovereignty and omniscience. Submission is not the act of submitting when it makes a person look good in front of others. Submission is not the act of submitting when it makes sense to the submitter. No. True submission is when your wife says, "Lord, You know my husband better than I do. I trust You, Lord, that he will be the husband, leader, provider, and protector that You have called him to be. I will pray for his wisdom and discernment all my days. My trust is ultimately in You, Lord, to lead him. May he heed Your voice, Lord."

Sin, whether it is yours or your wife's, may cause you to miss out on the blessings God originally had planned for your family.

He will allow you to experience whatever your obedience deserves. Rebekah had selfish desires for her favorite son. These desires created a division that is still felt today.

Again, may this serve as a warning. Sin creeps in. In the beginning of any relationship, we can truly be sincere in our faith. But if we are not diligent in seeking the Lord and heeding His commands for our life, we may become someone we don't recognize.

> Keep thy heart with all diligence; for out of it are
> the issues of life. (Proverbs 4:23)

CHAPTER 3

Joseph Resists Temptation

Genesis 39

And Joseph was brought down to Egypt; and Potiphar, an officer of Pharaoh, captain of the guard, an Egyptian, bought him of the hands of the Ishmaelites, which had brought him down thither. And the Lord was with Joseph, and he was a prosperous man; and he was in the house of his master the Egyptian. And his master saw that the Lord was with him, and that the Lord made all that he did to prosper in his hand. And Joseph found grace in his sight, and he served him: and he made him overseer over his house, and all that he had he put into his hand. And it came to pass from the time that he had made him overseer in his house, and over all that he had, that the Lord blessed the Egyptian's house for Joseph's sake; and the blessing of the Lord was upon all that he had in the house, and in the field. And he left all that he had in Joseph's hand; and he knew not ought he had, save the bread which he did eat. And Joseph was a goodly person, and well favoured. (Genesis 39:1–6)

Potiphar was the captain of the guard in Egypt. He was one of Pharaoh's officials. He was well-off, he had servants, and he was responsible for much. Potiphar was a successful man, yet he was not too prideful in his own successes to see the prosperity in Joseph's life. Potiphar recognized "that the Lord made all that [Joseph] did to prosper in his hand" (Genesis 39:3). He was humble enough to discern that Joseph's prosperity was not of his own making but was the result of God's blessings upon Joseph. He was wise enough to see that he should leave all that he had in Joseph's care. He acknowledged the Lord's favor being shown unto Joseph, not unto himself. It takes a truly humble man to recognize the importance of another man's character. Potiphar understood that the results of Joseph's actions were abundant blessings from the Lord. Most people want to take credit not only for their own prosperity but also for the prosperity of those around them, especially those under them. "And it came to pass from the time that he had made him overseer in his house, and over all that he had, that the Lord blessed the Egyptian's house for Joseph's sake; and the blessing of the Lord was upon all that he had in the house, and in the field" (Genesis 39:5). These blessings were not his own to claim.

Dear Son,

Please reflect on this. Let this sink in. Be humble enough to acknowledge the blessings of another. Be a man of integrity.

My son, I will say it again: it takes a truly humble man to acknowledge that his own success is not of his own making. A humble man is always willing to give the greater, more recognizable job to someone else. A humble man will recognize the works and efforts of those around him and under him. He will understand that his success depends on their success in their given duties. Son, I pray that you be this kind of man, humble, wise, thankful. I pray that you are able to look upon those who are less fortunate with eyes able to see the Lord's blessings upon them. This is a tremendous quality that will further your relationship with many people for Christ. Some of the happiest people in this world are those who have the least. Their treasure is not in material possessions but in eternal rewards. Joseph was not a man of prestige. He was a servant. Never let someone's circumstances alter your ability to see God's grace and blessing in their life.

I want you to look closely at this verse: "And he left all that he had in Joseph's hand; and he knew not ought he had, save the bread which he did eat. And Joseph was a goodly person, and well favoured" (Genesis 39:6). Potiphar left everything he had in Joseph's care. He no longer concerned himself with anything. I believe this was Potiphar's besetting sin. He became lazy. He was satisfied to live off the fat of Joseph's blessings. He no longer took care of his own responsibilities. Joseph was trustworthy, but Potiphar's wife was not. A man is to have full confidence in his wife, but even if she is trustworthy, he should not abandon his responsibilities as head of household, for that is the order God has ordained for a godly home. We must be good stewards of the gifts we have been given. Even though Potiphar had been given a tremendous gift in Joseph, he still had the responsibility of stewardship in how he spent his time, how he conducted his business, and how he ran his household. Even though he *was not* too prideful in his own abilities to allocate and delegate responsibilities to Joseph, he *was* too prideful in that he didn't think he could lose the blessings that had been bestowed upon him. He must have felt as though he had "made it." He was very prideful in thinking that what he possessed would always be his and that he would no longer have to work at it or maintain it. No matter how successful a man becomes or whether it be by his own making or the result of the efforts of others, he must continue, "whatsoever [he] do, [to] do it heartily, as to the Lord, and not unto men" (Colossians 3:23). This is true in work and in relationships. We must not become lazy in our efforts toward those He has given us to love, and we must not become lazy in our responsibilities. Even in success, our responsibilities do not diminish.

> And Joseph was a goodly person, and well favoured. And it came to pass after these things, that his master's wife cast her eyes upon Joseph; and she said, Lie with me. But he refused, and said unto his master's wife, Behold, my master wotteth not what is with me in the house, and he hath committed all that he hath to my hand; There is none greater in this house than I; neither hath he kept back any thing from me but thee, because thou art his wife: how then can I do this great wickedness, and sin against God? And it came to pass, as she spake to Joseph day by day, that he hearkened not unto her, to lie by her, or to be with her. (Genesis 39:6–10)

Potiphar's wife was obviously attracted to men in positions of power. After Joseph had been in charge for a while, she took note of how he looked and began to pursue him. My son, there are women like this. They are never satisfied with the man they have; they are always wanting more. Beware of this type of woman. Potiphar's wife was bold, saying, "Lie with me" (Genesis 39:7)! Joseph's response was an honorable one. He showed respect to both his master on earth and his Maker in heaven. Then he asked, "How then can I do this great wickedness, and sin against God" (Genesis 39:9)?

One important fact to note is Potiphar's discernment of Joseph's successes. It was obvious to Potiphar that the Lord was with Joseph. He saw that Joseph was a trustworthy servant and was honorable. Just as important to note is the fact that Potiphar's wife did not see the Lord's hand on Joseph. "The fool hath said in his heart, 'There is no God.' They are corrupt, they have done abominable works, there is none that doeth good" (Psalm 14:1). My dear son, one of the most difficult things to learn and apply to our way of thinking as Christians is that those who are not like us do not think like us. Being Christian, we automatically want to see the best in others. We have a Christlike love that desires to hope in all things. This is a wonderful quality, but sometimes it may skew our responsibility to discern. We must love but also be alert, astute, perceptive, and shrewd. Those who are not of God do not see our love with good intent, and they certainly do not see God's hand on us. Unless the Lord is drawing them to Him and has opened their eyes to His ways, they will misconstrue our intent as a plot to gain worldly treasures and pleasures. Potiphar's wife did not respect Joseph's authority as having come from the Lord, because she obviously did not respect or submit to her own husband's authority given to him by the Lord, or else she would not have been pursuing Joseph. Her eyes were blinded to the Lord's ways and His truth.

> And it came to pass about this time, that Joseph went into the house to do his business; and there

> was none of the men of the house there within.
> And she caught him by his garment, saying, Lie
> with me: and he left his garment in her hand, and
> fled, and got him out. (Genesis 39:11–12)

As Joseph repeatedly refused Potiphar's wife, she became even more determined. It became a manipulative pursuit. I don't know this to be true, but I would venture to guess that she thought that if the servants were out of the house, then he would have no reason not to sleep with her. I do not believe she could see his honorable refusal as truth. I believe she erroneously thought that he was only rejecting her so he would look good in front of the servants. She could not see his earnest and honest countenance to be true because she was manipulative herself. *Those who lie to get their own way believe others are doing the same. Untrustworthiness begets distrust in others.*

> And it came to pass, when she saw that he had
> left his garment in her hand, and was fled forth,
> That she called unto the men of her house, and
> spake unto them, saying, See, he hath brought in
> an Hebrew unto us to mock us; he came in unto
> me to lie with me, and I cried with a loud voice:
> And it came to pass, when he heard that I lifted up
> my voice and cried, that he left his garment with
> me, and fled, and got him out. (Genesis 39:13–15)

"When she saw that he had left his garment in her hand, and was fled forth" (Genesis 39:13). Either Potiphar's wife was offended at Joseph's complete rejection of her and became enraged because of it, or she knew that she would have to explain why she had his cloak. She refused to admit her pursuit of him, undermine her pride, or risk her own future, including her relationships with both the servants and Potiphar. In relation to the servants, she would have to trust and continue to trust that they would not betray the confidence she would be forced to place in them, relying on them never to reveal to Potiphar the circumstances of her betrayal. In relation to Potiphar, if he were to find out about her pursuit of Joseph, he could have her either put to death or put out.

> And she laid up his garment by her, until his lord came home. And she spake unto him according to these words, saying, The Hebrew servant, which thou hast brought unto us, came in unto me to mock me: And it came to pass, as I lifted up my voice and cried, that he left his garment with me, and fled out. And it came to pass, when his master heard the words of his wife, which she spake unto him, saying, After this manner did thy servant to me; that his wrath was kindled. And Joseph's master took him, and put him into the prison, a place where the king's prisoners were bound: and he was there in the prison. (Genesis 39:16–20)

In this rash moment, she made a decision that many manipulative people make—she decided to be a victim. *Conniving, manipulative, untrustworthy people are experts at making themselves the victims. Beware, my son, of these tactics.* Her pursuit of him turned into his pursuit of her. His honorable rejection of her turned into his having broken her honor. Joseph honored her by choosing not to disclose the details of her pursuit with Potiphar or the servants. He could have ruined her reputation, but he did not. Potiphar's wife's pursuit of Joseph turned into "Look at how your servant has treated me. ... He came in unto me to lie with me" (Genesis 39:14).

My son, I will say it again: beware of these tactics. There are many who behave this way. In your pursuit of marriage, "Watch ye, stand fast in the faith, quit you like men, be strong" (1 Corinthians 16:13). Be on your guard against such qualities as these. For those who are always finding fault in others, assuming the worst, and questioning others' motives, beware, for you will be at the receiving end of these tactics if you entangle yourself with a faultfinder. Pray for wisdom and discernment in pursuit of a wife. Look for someone who sees honesty as truth, godliness as honorable, and contentment as gain. Being with someone who is content in the Lord and content in her life will bring you much rest and happiness. "Keep thy heart with all diligence; for out of it are the issues of life" (Proverbs 4:23). In doing so, Son, you will find that in being with someone who sees love as love, kindness as kindness, and truth as truth, you will be guarding your heart against forming a critical spirit. If you are with someone with a critical spirit, you will grow to see things critically as well. Your joy for others will be discouraged and diminished. Again, pray for wisdom and discernment in this area.

Lessons from Potiphar

Potiphar was wise yet deceived. Remember, love covers a multitude of sins, but without proper discernment, it can cause you to erroneously overlook evil matters of the heart. For this reason, it is very important to be wise in your choosing of a wife. You must get to know a woman before you give your heart to her. Once you give your heart to her, the love in your heart for her will provoke you to excuse behaviors that otherwise would make you realize that she is not the one for you.

Potiphar was too trusting! Yes, we as Christians want to be trusting. We need to clothe ourselves in love and compassion each and every day, hoping for the best, keeping no record of wrongs, and enduring in our ways, but we also need not be too trusting of those with whom we should not entangle ourselves. Again, this is why it is of utmost importance not to give your heart to someone until you have prayed, observed, and received confirmation that she is who you believe her to be in a multitude of situations. *You learn more about a person's character when things go awry than when things are going well. Take your time.*

Potiphar was wise, yet he was not wise in choosing a wife. Pride comes before a fall. Yes, a man may be wise in many areas of his life, but if he has not been wise in choosing his wife, *he is not wise.* This is the most important decision you will ever make once you have chosen the Lord as your Savior. She, your wife, will be by your side for the rest of your life, making things either harder or easier to accomplish, making things have either more purpose or no purpose. And she has the ability to make things either more meaningful or meaningless. Her duty as a helpmeet is greater than you can imagine.

Life Application

I know of a woman who turned her family against her husband by only sharing half-truths about the arguments she'd had with him. She would describe him as abusive. In her attempts to make herself look like a better parent than he, she always talked about how much she did and minimize how much he did. Over a short period of time, her parents grew to hate him. The irony of it is that before she married, while she was dating the young man who would later become her husband, she'd described her family as abusive. She talked with him about how they'd mistreated her throughout her life. Even though they were kind to him while he was dating her, he was respectful but suspicious of them. She had only shared half-truths with him. Just a few years into their marriage, her husband and her family could hardly stand to be in the same room together. She now uses her turbulent family situation to victimize herself during prayer requests, work relationships, and affairs with other men. *Beware of those who share their misfortunes with you. Have a discerning spirit. There is a difference between sharing a terrible experience and victimizing yourself. Tears and drama do not always equate to a broken heart. A person who presents herself as a victim has a way of eventually finding fault with everyone in her life. A person whose heart has been broken because of abuse yet who is covered by God's grace will be able to share her experiences, possibly through tears, and will reveal God's work in her life and the lost condition of the soul who offended her.* Such a person has a heart broken by the sin but loves the sinner. There is a difference.

Life Application #2

This example in Genesis serves to warn a man never to be alone with a woman who is not his blood relative or wife. Always be in the open together so no woman can wrongly accuse you of any misbehavior. Be vigilant about this, my son. Never assume that it would never happen to you. Not only are you protecting yourself, but also you are protecting the woman's reputation. Don't allow her to be a subject of gossip where others would have an opportunity to say of her, "She went into his office behind closed doors, or into his home, for [this length of time]," etc. You are also protecting yourself from any possible temptation. You must make it a habit for each encounter with someone of the opposite sex not to close the door of the room you are in. This serves to let others know that they are welcome to come in or see what is going on between the two of you because there is nothing hidden or secret about the goings-on between you. If you find yourself in a job that allows you the opportunity to go into people's homes, make sure you stay outside. If the job is one where you must go inside, try to have a helper with you. If you must be alone, do not engage in conversation with the woman other than to discuss the specific purpose for which you are there. If your job entails going to lunch with customers, and if the customer is a female, you must make it a practice to invite another person to come to lunch with the two of you. These are just good practices that must be exercised in order to protect your reputation as well as the woman's reputation.

Dear Lord,

I pray that my son will seek you as his guide throughout his life. Each place you move his feet to tread, there is no accidental encounter. He does not know who You have planned for him, but, Lord, I pray that You draw him to You and to Your choice of a wife for him. There are many men who fully trust in their wives, and that should be a welcome gift in their marriage. Unfortunately, if the man has not chosen a trustworthy wife, she may victimize herself and turn him away from those You want to use to bring blessings to his life. Dear Lord, I pray that my son remembers to place his trust in You at all times. I pray that he finds a wife in whom he will be able to have full confidence and that she will bring him peace, not evil, all the days of his life (Jeremiah 29:11). May he recognize the importance of her character, and may she be not selfish but selfless—thinking of others, not using others in order to get her way. May You grant my son wisdom and discernment. May You lead him to the lady You have set out just for him.

In Jesus's name, I pray. Amen

CHAPTER 4

Samson and His Wives—Not Just Delilah

Judges 13

And the children of Israel did evil again in the sight of the Lord; and the Lord delivered them into the hand of the Philistines forty years. And there was a certain man of Zorah, of the family of the Danites, whose name was Manoah; and his wife was barren, and bare not. And the angel of the Lord appeared unto the woman, and said unto her, Behold now, thou art barren, and bearest not: but

thou shalt conceive, and bear a son. Now therefore
beware, I pray thee, and drink not wine nor strong
drink, and eat not any unclean thing: For, lo, thou
shalt conceive, and bear a son; and no razor shall
come on his head: for the child shall be a Nazarite
unto God from the womb: and he shall begin to
deliver Israel out of the hand of the Philistines.
Then the woman came and told her husband,
saying, A man of God came unto me, and his
countenance was like the countenance of an angel
of God, very terrible: but I asked him not whence
he was, neither told he me his name: But he said
unto me, Behold, thou shalt conceive, and bear
a son; and now drink no wine nor strong drink,
neither eat any unclean thing: for the child shall
be a Nazarite to God from the womb to the day
of his death. Then Manoah intreated the Lord,
and said, O my Lord, let the man of God which
thou didst send come again unto us, and teach us
what we shall do unto the child that shall be born.
And God hearkened to the voice of Manoah; and
the angel of God came again unto the woman as
she sat in the field: but Manoah her husband was
not with her. And the woman made haste, and
ran, and shewed her husband, and said unto him,
Behold, the man hath appeared unto me, that
came unto me the other day. And Manoah arose,
and went after his wife, and came to the man,
and said unto him, Art thou the man that spakest
unto the woman? And he said, I am. And Manoah
said, Now let thy words come to pass. How shall
we order the child, and how shall we do unto him?
And the angel of the Lord said unto Manoah, Of
all that I said unto the woman let her beware.

She may not eat of any thing that cometh of the vine, neither let her drink wine or strong drink, nor eat any unclean thing: all that I commanded her let her observe. And Manoah said unto the angel of the Lord, I pray thee, let us detain thee, until we shall have made ready a kid for thee. And the angel of the Lord said unto Manoah, Though thou detain me, I will not eat of thy bread: and if thou wilt offer a burnt offering, thou must offer it unto the Lord. For Manoah knew not that he was an angel of the Lord. And Manoah said unto the angel of the Lord, What is thy name, that when thy sayings come to pass we may do thee honour? And the angel of the Lord said unto him, Why askest thou thus after my name, seeing it is secret? So Manoah took a kid with a meat offering, and offered it upon a rock unto the Lord: and the angel did wonderously; and Manoah and his wife looked on. For it came to pass, when the flame went up toward heaven from off the altar, that the angel of the Lord ascended in the flame of the altar. And Manoah and his wife looked on it, and fell on their faces to the ground. But the angel of the Lord did no more appear to Manoah and to his wife. Then Manoah knew that he was an angel of the Lord. And Manoah said unto his wife, We shall surely die, because we have seen God. But his wife said unto him, If the Lord were pleased to kill us, he would not have received a burnt offering and a meat offering at our hands, neither would he have shewed us all these things, nor would as at this time have told us such things as these. And the woman bare a son, and called his name Samson: and the child grew, and the Lord blessed him. And

the Spirit of the Lord began to move him at times
in the camp of Dan between Zorah and Eshtaol.
(Judges 13:1–25)

In this passage, Manoah doesn't recognize the man as a man of God. Manoah wanted to give the *man* honor by offering him sacrifices.[7] The man of God told Manoah to offer the sacrifice to the Lord. He was pointing Manoah to the Father, but Manoah wanted to give thanks to the man. He never recognized that he should be giving thanks to the Lord. Manoah's wife knew the man had been sent to her by the Lord. Manoah's action here is an example of the father's sin. The father is charged with the responsibility of leading the household. *This father should have been able to recognize the work of the Lord.* Being the spiritual leader of the home is a responsibility not to be taken lightly. "The Lord is longsuffering, and of great mercy, forgiving iniquity and transgression, and by no means clearing the guilty, visiting the iniquity of the fathers upon the children unto the third and fourth generation" (Numbers 14:18). You will see in the next passages that the sin of exalting man and not offering sacrifices to the Lord is passed onto the next generation.

Judges 14

And Samson went down to Timnath, and saw a woman in Timnath of the daughters of the Philistines. And he came up, and told his father and his mother, and said, I have seen a woman in Timnath of the daughters of the Philistines: now therefore get her for me to wife. Then his father and his mother said unto him, Is there never a woman

---

[7] Warren Wiersbe, *Bible Commentary: Old Testament* (Nashville: Thomas Nelson, 1991).

among the daughters of thy brethren, or among all
my people, that thou goest to take a wife of the
uncircumcised Philistines? And Samson said unto
his father, Get her for me; for she pleaseth me well.
But his father and his mother knew not that it was
of the Lord, that he sought an occasion against
the Philistines: for at that time the Philistines had
dominion over Israel. (Judges 14:1–4)

The demanding and disrespectful nature evident in Samson's
attitude toward his parents and within his own will is evident.
In Deuteronomy 7:3–4, the Lord commands the Israelites not
to marry the enemy but to destroy them all. In Judges 14:4, the
Bible tells us that this desire to be entangled with the enemy was
emplaced by the Lord because He was seeking an occasion to
confront the Philistines. I believe God chose Samson because he
was usable. Samson's pride, his selfishness, and the weakness of his
parents were perfect traits that made him both usable and suitable
for a confrontation with the enemy.

Then went Samson down, and his father and his
mother, to Timnath, and came to the vineyards of
Timnath: and, behold, a young lion roared against
him. And the Spirit of the Lord came mightily
upon him, and he rent him as he would have rent
a kid, and he had nothing in his hand: but he told
not his father or his mother what he had done.
And he went down, and talked with the woman;
and she pleased Samson well. And after a time
he returned to take her, and he turned aside to
see the carcase of the lion: and, behold, there was
a swarm of bees and honey in the carcase of the
lion. And he took thereof in his hands, and went
on eating, and came to his father and mother,

and he gave them, and they did eat: but he told
not them that he had taken the honey out of the
carcase of the lion. (Judges 14:5–9)

We see in verse 6 that Samson was given power by the Lord to kill
a young lion. "Your adversary the devil, as a roaring lion, walketh
about, seeking whom he may devour: Whom resist steadfast in
the faith" (1 Peter 5:8–9a). I don't know if this lion is symbolic of
the prowling lion in the foregoing verse, but Samson did not resist
it. He took it on. He was given power by the Lord to conquer the
lion, but it served as an invitation to Samson to become entangled
with the enemy. He did not confide in his parents his deeds. He
continued with his plan to marry into the family of the enemy. As
he went to marry the woman, he defiled himself by touching the
unclean meat and partaking of the spoils that remained there long
enough for bees to harvest honey within the carcass. He was willing
to defile himself for a taste of honey. He was bold in his lack of self-
control. With no shame in the act of defiling himself, he shared this
honey with his parents without telling them from where it came.
When you allow yourself to partake in sin, you want to bring others
with you; it makes you feel justified in your sin. One may think,
It is not so bad. It didn't hurt any of us to eat the honey. No, it didn't
hurt any of them to eat the honey, *not immediately! But* the inward
decay began. The man was no longer looking to the Lord for what
is right and wrong, but he looked from side to side to judge that
he was better than this person but not as bad as that person, so
his sin wasn't so bad—which is a lie! Looking around you is a trap.
You will always find someone worse than you, thus causing you to
think more highly of yourself than you ought. And you will always
find someone better than you, thus causing you to think worse of
yourself than you ought, filling your heart with self-doubt or defeat.

So his father went down unto the woman: and
Samson made there a feast; for so used the young

men to do. And it came to pass, when they saw him, that they brought thirty companions to be with him. And Samson said unto them, I will now put forth a riddle unto you: if ye can certainly declare it me within the seven days of the feast, and find it out, then I will give you thirty sheets and thirty change of garments: But if ye cannot declare it me, then shall ye give me thirty sheets and thirty change of garments. And they said unto him, Put forth thy riddle, that we may hear it. (Judges 14:10–13)

Here we see Samson's pride once again. He believed he could outsmart thirty men. He did not have his wife's heart. He could not fully trust in her, but his pride did not allow him to see his own weakness.

And he said unto them, Out of the eater came forth meat, and out of the strong came forth sweetness. And they could not in three days expound the riddle. And it came to pass on the seventh day, that they said unto Samson's wife, Entice thy husband, that he may declare unto us the riddle, lest we burn thee and thy father's house with fire: have ye called us to take that we have? is it not so? And Samson's wife wept before him, and said, Thou dost but hate me, and lovest me not: thou hast put forth a riddle unto the children of my people, and hast not told it me. And he said unto her, Behold, I have not told it my father nor my mother, and shall I tell it thee? (Judges 14:14–16)

A husband must fulfill his role as protector. When a husband fulfills his role as protector, his wife sees his position as a source of comfort and security. She readily wants to be identified as his. She will look to him, and her heart will desire to be viewed as one with his. They are no longer two but as one. They are family. Samson did not protect his wife from others. He allowed her to be alone with these companions long enough for them to threaten her. They convinced her to coax him into telling her the answer to his riddle. Her heart was not his. She was more concerned for herself and for her own people, which is a common trait in a wife who does not feel protected by her husband. She did not see Samson as her family. She was not concerned for them in their roles as husband and wife, as a family, but was only concerned for her own family of origin, the family from which she came. She threw herself on him. She sobbed. She accused him of not really loving her. She tried manipulative tactics such as "You've given my people a riddle, but you haven't even told me the answer," which I translate into, "Aren't I more important to you than they?"

> Behold, I have not told it my father nor my mother, and shall I tell it thee? And she wept before him the seven days, while their feast lasted: and it came to pass on the seventh day, that he told her, because she lay sore upon him: and she told the riddle to the children of her people. (Judges 14:16b–17)

He didn't look into her ways. He did not suspect that she had ulterior motives for seeking the answer to his riddle. He merely responded, "I haven't even told my parents, so why should I explain it to you?" This statement is so telling of his character. He unashamedly admitted that he had never even submitted to the authority of his parents or respected his parents' position, so why should he now have to be held accountable to his wife? He did not see their union as a union blessed by God. He did not see his responsibility as her husband to love her and to protect her. His lust for her in his pursuit of her was not indicative of his having desired a loving, respectful union. She was an object that he conquered. He erroneously believed that he had conquered his pursuit. He saw himself in a position of power, not in a position of weakness. He was deceived. If you let your heart turn to lust or be turned toward the enemy, and if your pride prevents you from seeing the mistakes you've made or the position of weakness you've allowed yourself to be in, then you are doomed to deeper and deeper pitfalls of sin.

After allowing his wife to plead and cry for seven days, Samson broke down and told her the answer to his riddle. Now, whether he just got tired of listening to her or he felt sorry for her, he decided to confide in her the answer to his riddle. He nevertheless placed his trust, once again, in the wrong place. First, because of his pride, he placed his trust in his own ability, but now he erroneously placed his trust in his wife.

> And the men of the city said unto him on the seventh day before the sun went down, "What is sweeter than honey? And what is stronger than a lion?" and he said unto them, "If ye had not plowed with my heifer, ye had not found out my riddle." And the Spirit of the Lord came upon him, and he went down to Ashkelon, and slew thirty men of them, and took their spoil, and gave change of garments unto them which expounded the riddle. And his anger was kindled, and he went up to his father's house. But Samson's wife was given to his companion, whom he had used as his friend. (Judges 14:18–20)

Before the day was over, the men answered Samson's riddle. Once again, instead of Samson recognizing his own sin and admitting he had been deceived by his wife, he blamed the men for messing with his wife. He was angry at everyone but himself. He thought more highly of himself than he ought to have. "For I say, through the grace given unto me, to every man that is among you, not to think of himself more highly than he ought to think; but to think soberly, according as God hath dealt to every man the measure of faith" (Romans 12:3).

He left the situation and went home, leaving his wife unattended and unprotected. He lost her to another man because of his own anger.

Pride causes you not to be able to recognize your own sin, confess it, or repent of it. It causes bitterness and unforgiveness. Pride hardens your heart toward others, and it hardens your heart in its ability to recognize its own sin. "And why beholdest thou the mote that is in thy brother's eye, but considerest not the beam that is in thine own eye" (Matthew 7:3)?

Judges 15

But it came to pass within a while after, in the time of wheat harvest, that Samson visited his wife with a kid; and he said, I will go in to my wife into the chamber. But her father would not suffer him to go in. And her father said, I verily thought that thou hadst utterly hated her; therefore I gave her to thy companion: is not her younger sister fairer than she? take her, I pray thee, instead of her. And Samson said concerning them, Now shall I be more blameless than the Philistines, though I do them a displeasure. And Samson went and caught three hundred foxes, and took firebrands, and turned tail to tail, and put a firebrand in the midst between two tails. And when he had set the brands on fire, he let them go into the standing corn of the Philistines, and burnt up both the

shocks, and also the standing corn, with the
vineyards and olives. (Judges 15:1–5)

Samson, out of his anger about losing his wife, destroyed many
things that were not his to destroy. Yes, they were the enemy's
things, but they had not caused his heartache. His own sin of
pride and anger caused his trouble. Beware, my son, of turning
your heart toward the wrong woman, because once it is turned,
you will have the strong emotions of a warrior/protector/provider
that sometimes overrule any type of common sense.

Samson's reaction to his wife being given to another man
caused her death as well as her father's death. Samson once again
saw their sin, not his own. In verse 7, *Samson was basically saying to
them, "Since you've acted like this, I swear that I won't stop until I get
my revenge on you."* He justified his actions by citing their actions.

Later on … Samson went to visit his wife. (Judges
15:1)

Samson left his wife. Prideful people almost always assume that no
matter what type of behavior they have exercised in the past, their
own people will always be there when they are ready to come back
to the relationship. They take their family for granted, assuming
that when they are ready to come back, they can pick up where
they left off. They erroneously expect those whom they left to be
waiting for them and assume that they will be thankful for their
return. But Samson's wife had been given away. She was no longer
in need of him. She had been given to another man to have her.
Samson mistakenly thought he now had the right to come back,
most likely because *he* had cooled off. But his neglect in fulfilling
his duties as protector caused him to lose any benefit of being her
husband.

My son, this is why it is so important to stay in a state of
thankfulness. Always remember that what you have is on loan to

you from the Creator of it *all*! What has been given can be taken away. Don't be foolish in relying on your own strength, your own ability, and your own family for your needs. God is the source of all our needs. Be thankful for everything you have been given to the One who has abundantly given.

> Then the Philistines said, Who hath done this? And they answered, Samson, the son in law of the Timnite, because he had taken his wife, and given her to his companion. And the Philistines came up, and burnt her and her father with fire. And Samson said unto them, Though ye have done this, yet will I be avenged of you, and after that I will cease. And he smote them hip and thigh with a great slaughter: and he went down and dwelt in the top of the rock Etam. (Judges 15:6–8)

Samson's wife pressed him. It seemed like he hated her, yet he was still willing to kill for her. Once your heart is turned toward another's, you are entangled. This is one of the many reasons why you must be cautious about to whom you give your heart.

> Then the Philistines went up, and pitched in Judah, and spread themselves in Lehi. And the men of Judah said, Why are ye come up against us? And they answered, To bind Samson are we come up, to do to him as he hath done to us. Then three thousand men of Judah went to the top of the rock Etam, and said to Samson, Knowest thou not that the Philistines are rulers over us? what is this that thou hast done unto us? And he said unto them, As they did unto me, so have I done unto them. (Judges 15:9–11)

One man's sin (vengeance) affects not only him but also those around him. It causes others to suffer and to fear the consequences of his sin. Your sin is not your own.

> And they said unto him, We are come down to bind thee, that we may deliver thee into the hand of the Philistines. And Samson said unto them, Swear unto me, that ye will not fall upon me yourselves. And they spake unto him, saying, No; but we will bind thee fast, and deliver thee into their hand: but surely we will not kill thee. And they bound him with two new cords, and brought him up from the rock. And when he came unto Lehi, the Philistines shouted against him: and the Spirit of the Lord came mightily upon him, and the cords that were upon his arms became as flax that was burnt with fire, and his bands loosed from off his hands. And he found a new jawbone of an ass, and put forth his hand, and took it, and slew a thousand men therewith. And Samson said, With the jawbone of an ass, heaps upon heaps, with the jaw of an ass have I slain a thousand men. And it came to pass, when he had made an end of speaking, that he cast away the jawbone out of his hand, and called that place Ramathlehi. And he was sore athirst, and called on the Lord, and said, Thou hast given this great deliverance into the hand of thy servant: and now shall I die for thirst, and fall into the hand of the uncircumcised? But God clave an hollow place that was in the jaw, and there came water thereout; and when he had drunk, his spirit came again, and he revived: wherefore he called the name thereof Enhakkore,

which is in Lehi unto this day. And he judged Israel in the days of the Philistines twenty years. (Judges 15:12–20)

Judges 16

Then went Samson to Gaza, and saw there an harlot, and went in unto her. And it was told the Gazites, saying, Samson is come hither. And they compassed him in, and laid wait for him all night in the gate of the city, and were quiet all the night, saying, In the morning, when it is day, we shall kill him. And Samson lay till midnight, and arose at midnight, and took the doors of the gate of the city, and the two posts, and went away with them, bar and all, and put them upon his shoulders, and carried them up to the top of an hill that is before Hebron. And it came to pass afterward, that he loved a woman in the valley of Sorek, whose name was Delilah. (Judges 16:1–4)

When you make a habit of entangling yourself with those who sell themselves for money, with those who daily make dishonest deals because of their greed for money, and with those who show a pattern of dishonesty and selfish gain, you learn to play the worldly games they play. *You entertain their ploys because of your secret weaknesses*, but after lying day after day and night after night, sharing the most intimate part of yourself with one who is untrustworthy, you erroneously begin to trust that she truly *does* care about you. You see her ploys as an innocent game. You are no longer able to discern the dishonesty and the plot behind the evil motives.

If you surround yourself with prostitutes, ones who sell their souls for temporary gain and ones who don't respect the gifts they've been given, then you become like them. Samson became the same as the one with whom he had lain. He did not respect his gift of strength as something that had been given to him from the Lord. He pridefully thought it was *his* talent to be used for his own gain. *His father's sin had fallen upon him.* Manoah did not see the blessing on his family as a gift from God but as a gift from man, and now Samson failed to see the blessing he had been given as a gift from God. Manoah wanted to pay tribute to the man, not to God. Now, Samson did not recognize his gift of strength as a source of power from the Lord, but he saw his strength as stemming from his own ability as a man. Samson sold his gift in exchange for temporary relief from his human tiredness. He was not relying on the Lord's strength; he was relying on his own might and power. "The joy of the Lord is your strength" (Nehemiah 8:10). Samson's joy was in his own accomplishments—not in what the Lord had done through him.

Manoah allowed his son to have too much authority in their house, not teaching his son to be a leader in submission to the Lord. Instead he submitted to his son's demands and disrespect, thereby creating the perfect backdrop for a life full of pride and self-centeredness in his son's heart. With these qualities, Samson became the perfect person for the Lord to use for His cause against the Philistines. My son, may you never be found to be the perfect person the Lord can use to become entangled with the enemy. May it be your desire to be the perfect person the Lord can use to bring about joy and peace.

He Fell in Love

> And it came to pass afterward, that he loved a woman in the valley of Sorek, whose name was Delilah. And the lords of the Philistines came up unto her, and said unto her, Entice him, and see wherein his great strength lieth, and by what

> means we may prevail against him, that we may bind him to afflict him; and we will give thee every one of us eleven hundred pieces of silver. And Delilah said to Samson, Tell me, I pray thee, wherein thy great strength lieth, and wherewith thou mightest be bound to afflict thee. (Judges 16:4–6)

Samson fell in love with a woman in the valley of Sorek. After Samson continuously had the wrong relationships with the wrong kind of women, he now had fallen truly in love with one who was not his own. She was the enemy. The Philistines knew that she was the perfect tool for them to use to get him to reveal his secret. The Philistines knew she would be willing to lure him for money. In Samson's relationship with Delilah, he was not honest with her either. He told her things to appease her desire to find out the source of his strength yet never revealed the truth behind his power. By this time, Samson had become so accustomed to being in relationships with women who had ulterior motives that he didn't see it as anything less than the nature of relationships. It is obvious that he did not completely trust Delilah, yet each time he told her what the source of his strength was, she tried to capture him using the tactics that he had told her would take away his strength. Instead of Samson being alarmed by her wicked ways and seeing that she was trying to trap him, he continued in his relationship with her. Once she saw that her schemes did not work, she immediately portrayed herself as the victim of his lies. She began telling him his wrongs against her and began to make him feel responsible for her unhappiness. She used tactics like "You have made a fool of me," when in actuality she was making a fool of *him* all along. My son, beware of ones who are constant victims. Never underestimate the lures of this type of woman and her power to control your actions. When you lie with a woman, you are sharing an intimate, private part of yourself that automatically conveys your vulnerability to her, which is why it is so important not to give your heart away to someone who is not trustworthy, honorable, and sincere in her faith in the Lord and her love for you.

> And Samson said unto her, If they bind me with seven green withs that were never dried, then shall I be weak, and be as another man. Then the lords of the Philistines brought up to her seven green withs which had not been dried, and she bound him with them. Now there were men lying in wait, abiding with her in the chamber. And she said unto him, The Philistines be upon thee, Samson. And he brake the withs, as a thread of tow is broken when it toucheth the fire. So his strength was not known. And Delilah said unto Samson, Behold, thou hast mocked me, and told me lies: now tell me, I pray thee, wherewith thou mightest be bound. And he said unto her, If they bind me fast with new ropes that never were occupied, then shall I be weak, and be as another man. Delilah therefore took new ropes, and bound him therewith, and said unto him, The Philistines be upon thee, Samson. And there were liers in wait abiding in the chamber. And he brake them from off his arms like a thread. And Delilah said unto Samson, Hitherto thou hast mocked me, and told me lies: tell me wherewith thou mightest be bound. And he said unto her, If thou weavest the seven locks of my head with the web. And she fastened it with the pin, and said unto him, The Philistines be upon thee, Samson. And he awaked out of his sleep, and went away with the pin of the beam, and with the web. (Judges 16:7–14)

Samson never addressed Delilah's proclamations of, "The Philistines be upon thee" (Judges 16:14)! Always remember that in love you assume the best in others, but be wise always to find the truth of a matter. Test the spirit of the person. If the person continually does things that could cause you harm, or if she is constantly testing your authenticity, then you must begin to start questioning her motives.

> And she said unto him, How canst thou say, I love thee, when thine heart is not with me? thou hast mocked me these three times, and hast not told me wherein thy great strength lieth. And it came to pass, when she pressed him daily with her words, and urged him, so that his soul was vexed unto death; That he told her all his heart, and said unto her, There hath not come a razor upon mine head; for I have been a Nazarite unto God from my mother's womb: if I be shaven, then my strength will go from me, and I shall become weak, and be like any other man. And when Delilah saw that he had told her all his heart, she sent and called for the lords of the Philistines, saying, Come up this once, for he hath shewed me all his heart. Then the lords of the Philistines came up unto her, and brought money in their hand. And she made him sleep upon her knees; and she called for a man, and she caused him to shave off the seven locks of his head; and she began to afflict him, and his strength went from him. And she said, The Philistines be upon thee, Samson. And he awoke out of his sleep, and said, I will go out as at other times before, and shake myself. And he wist not that the Lord was departed from him. But the Philistines took him, and put out his eyes,

and brought him down to Gaza, and bound him with fetters of brass; and he did grind in the prison house. (Judges 16:15–21)

How canst thou say, "I love thee"? (Judges 16:15)

How can you say "I love you" when you won't confide in me? This is manipulation. How could Delilah speak of true love when she had none to give? She tired Samson out and nagged him until he was worn out. When he did sincerely confide in her, he had lost sight of her dishonesty. I think he erroneously believed she would see his sincerity and then be true to him. She *did* recognize his sincerity. "And when Delilah saw that he had told her all his heart, she sent and called for the lords of the Philistines, saying, Come up this once, for he hath shewed me all his heart" (Judges 16:18). *She saw his sincerity and used it for her own gain.* People who are filled with sin, who do not have the joy of the Lord, and who do not possess His love in their hearts do not see sincerity and kindness for what those qualities are. They see sincerity and kindness as weakness. When you lie with one who sells/gives away her soul, know that she has no respect for herself or for you and your feelings. Samson had been raised to know the truth. Deep within his heart, he knew the truth. He chose to play with fire, and he got burned. He expected that deep down she knew the same truths that he knew to be true within his own heart, but she had not been brought up in the same manner. The truth was not within her. Sincerity was not in her heart. Because neither the truth nor sincerity resided in her heart, those traits were not recognizable to her. Those traits were tools to be used by her in order to further her cause.

"And she made him sleep upon her knees" (Judges 16:19). When a woman offers her lap for a man to rest his head, there is an understood compassion in that gesture. This gesture to lie down says, *Come and rest. I understand that you have been through much, and I will nurture you by letting you sleep in the comfort of my maternal lap.* As Samson fell asleep there, Delilah did not soften to his vulnerability. She did not see his needs. She saw an advantage, the opportunity she had been waiting for. She called a man to shave Samson's head and to have him subdued. She did not have remorse. Let's think about this for a moment. The only other woman in a man's life to offer her lap for him to lay his head upon is his mother. In Delilah's case, this was a very manipulative gesture. Samson laid his head down upon her lap. She was most likely stroking his face or shoulders or back while he was drifting off to sleep. She watched him trustfully fall asleep, into a state of vulnerability. Did she then feel remorse? No. She did as she had always done and called to him, "The Philistines be upon thee, Samson" (Judges 16:20).

"He awoke out of his sleep and said, 'I will go out as at other times before, and shake myself'" (Judges 16:20). He thought he would be able to go out as before. He still didn't fully recognize who or how powerful the enemy was. He never saw that he had placed himself in a position of weakness. Because he had always been able to get away with his sin, he believed he would continue to be able to get away with it. Satan will deceive you into thinking your wisdom and your ability to navigate through your life is all you need to get you through life's trials, but without the Lord as your guide, the strength you need to make wise choices will fail you.

When you are married, there will be times when you will need the other person to care for you. You will rely on her to regard your best interests as her best interests. Make sure you are with someone who is not in it for herself. Make sure she is someone who is willing to fight for you and your well-being. You want someone who is not always thinking of herself and her costs but someone who willingly serves others, who looks outside herself, and who sacrificially loves.

But the Philistines took him, and put out his eyes,
and brought him down to Gaza, and bound him

with fetters of brass; and he did grind in the prison house. Howbeit the hair of his head began to grow again after he was shaven. Then the lords of the Philistines gathered them together for to offer a great sacrifice unto Dagon their god, and to rejoice: for they said, Our god hath delivered Samson our enemy into our hand. And when the people saw him, they praised their god: for they said, Our god hath delivered into our hands our enemy, and the destroyer of our country, which slew many of us. And it came to pass, when their hearts were merry, that they said, Call for Samson, that he may make us sport. And they called for Samson out of the prison house; and he made them sport: and they set him between the pillars. And Samson said unto the lad that held him by the hand, Suffer me that I may feel the pillars whereupon the house standeth, that I may lean upon them. Now the house was full of men and women; and all the lords of the Philistines were there; and there were upon the roof about three thousand men and women, that beheld while Samson made sport. And Samson called unto the Lord, and said, O Lord God, remember me, I pray thee, and strengthen me, I pray thee, only this once, O God, that I may be at once avenged of the Philistines for my two eyes. And Samson took hold of the two middle pillars upon which the house stood, and on which it was borne up, of the one with his right hand, and of the other with his left. And Samson said, Let me die with the Philistines. And he bowed himself with all his might; and the house fell upon the lords, and upon all the people that were therein. So the dead which he slew at his death were more than they which he slew in his life. Then his brethren and all the house of his father came down, and took him, and brought him up, and buried him between Zorah and Eshtaol in the buryingplace of Manoah his father. And he judged Israel twenty years. (Judges 16:21–31)

"Samson said, 'Let me die with the Philistines'" (Judges 16:30). He lay with the enemy time and time again until the Lord left him to his own devices. He was overtaken by the enemy and then used for their entertainment. Not only did he want vengeance for their actions against him, but also he wanted to die with them. He fully recognized that he had entangled himself with them in life and that he was not worthy to be disentangled from them in death. Sin will take you farther than you want to go, keep you there longer than you want to stay, and cost you more than you want to pay. "He, that being often reproved hardeneth his neck, shall suddenly be destroyed, and that without remedy" (Proverbs 29:1).

I believe Samson saw the depths of his own sin while he was being made to entertain the crowd. He saw the same selfishness in them that he had exercised throughout his life. Both the Philistines and Samson only thought of what they wanted, never thinking of others' needs or the costs of their desires. The Philistines wanted to be entertained by him, just as he wanted to be entertained by ungodly women. They wanted him to be on display as an example of their power and strength, just as he wanted to display his ability to conquer through his power and strength. He never cared about his parents, nor did he seek or rely on the Lord in any way. He identified his sin in their sin and knew he did not deserve a death any different from theirs because he had lain with the enemy and had made himself no different.

Dear Lord,

I pray that my son beware of a prideful nature taking root in his heart. I pray that he make it a daily habit to pray "and see if there be any wicked way in [him], and [that You] lead [him] in the way everlasting" (Psalm 139:24). Lord, as the song says, "It is a slow fade."[8] Please, help my son to be discerning in all his ways. May he prepare himself and strive to have qualities that will enable him to be the husband he needs to be, not just looking for the qualities in a wife that he needs and desires. Lord, help him to recognize the enemy. Please do not allow him to make himself a usable instrument who will become entangled with the enemy. Lord, I pray that when he is tempted, he will flee. Lord, the days are evil, and immorality is rampant. Women dress in ways in which they have never dressed before. Lord, as Brother Greg Butler has stated, a man cannot control what he sees, but he can control what he gazes upon.[9] Lord, I pray that as my son grows more fully into manhood and no longer has his parents to help filter out the evils of the world, he will guard his heart and be the filter for himself that sees evil as evil and good as good. Lord, I pray that You help him to continue to be vigilant in a constant pursuit of righteousness. May he be the husband that a godly wife would be blessed to have. In Jesus's name, I pray. Amen.

---

[8] Casting Crowns, "Slow Fade," by Mark Hall, recorded 2008, track 3 on *The Altar and the Door*, Beach Street, Reunion.

[9] Greg Butler, pastor, Bible Baptist Church of Monroe, ww.biblebapt.org.

CHAPTER 5

A man is to be like Joseph, Jesus's earthly father.

This chapter was written and completely inspired by the Lord through the preaching and teaching by Brother Greg Butler, my pastor at Bible Baptist Church in Monroe, Georgia, whose permission I have to make use of his sermons.

Matthew 1

> Now the birth of Jesus Christ was on this wise:
> When as his mother Mary was espoused to
> Joseph, before they came together, she was found
> with child of the Holy Ghost. Then Joseph her

husband, being a just man, and not willing to make her a public example, was minded to put her away privily. But while he thought on these things, behold, the angel of the Lord appeared unto him in a dream, saying, Joseph, thou son of David, fear not to take unto thee Mary thy wife: for that which is conceived in her is of the Holy Ghost. And she shall bring forth a son, and thou shalt call his name Jesus: for he shall save his people from their sins. (Matthew 1:18–21)

Not only did God choose Mary because she was found to be a pure servant, obedient and humble, but also Joseph was chosen to be Jesus's earthly father because *he was a righteous man*. Being righteous, Joseph sought to do what was right in the eyes of the Lord. Even upon finding out that Mary was with child, he had a protective love for her as he did not want to expose her sin. He did not want to publicly disgrace her. He was loyal even when he questioned her faithfulness to him. He had it in his mind to divorce her quietly. True love covers a multitude of sins. It overlooks wrongs that have been done and hopes for what is best.

Joseph was also *a thoughtful man*. He was not rash in his decision-making. He was not quickly provoked. "But while he thought on these things, behold, the angel of the Lord appeared unto him in a dream, saying, Joseph, thou son of David, fear not to take unto thee Mary thy wife: for that which is conceived in her is of the Holy Ghost" (Matthew 1:20).

Now all this was done, that it might be fulfilled which was spoken of the Lord by the prophet, saying, Behold, a virgin shall be with child, and shall bring forth a son, and they shall call his name Emmanuel, which being interpreted is, God with us. Then Joseph being raised from sleep did

as the angel of the Lord had bidden him, and took
unto him his wife: And knew her not till she had
brought forth her firstborn son: and he called his
name Jesus. (Matthew 1:22–25)

Joseph was an attentive man. He was seeking the Lord's direction
for his life. When he had these dreams, he did not discount them.
He recognized them as the Lord's commands for his life and the
lives of his family members. "My sheep hear my voice, and I know
them, and they follow me" (John 10:27).

Verse 24 says that he was *an obedient man.* "He did as the
angel of the Lord had bidden him" (Matthew 1:24). He was *a
self-controlled man.* In verse 25 it tells how he had no union with
Mary until she gave birth to a son. He was given the privilege to
name the Savior of the World—"and he called his name Jesus"
(Matthew 1:25).

Matthew 2

And when they were departed, behold, the angel
of the Lord appeareth to Joseph in a dream, saying,
Arise, and take the young child and his mother,
and flee into Egypt, and be thou there until I bring
thee word: for Herod will seek the young child to
destroy him. When he arose, he took the young
child and his mother by night, and departed into
Egypt: And was there until the death of Herod:
that it might be fulfilled which was spoken of the
Lord by the prophet, saying, Out of Egypt have I
called my son. (Matthew 2:13–15)

Joseph was a protector. A man cannot be both apathetic and a
protector. Apathy says, "Surely there is no imminent danger. I need
proof. I will wait until I see the enemy approaching." A protector

warrior says, "I must be prudent. I must be proactive, not reactive. This is for the welfare of my family. I will heed the warnings. I do not need to wait for proof." In addition, when Joseph learned that his and Mary's life was going to be filled with persecution, that there were threats on their very lives, he did not cower. He did not back down from his responsibilities. He did not leave Mary and say, "This is not my son." He faced his responsibilities with courage. He followed God's direction with a submissive spirit, fulfilling the purposes for his life and his new family's life.

> But when Herod was dead, behold, an angel of the Lord appeareth in a dream to Joseph in Egypt, Saying, Arise, and take the young child and his mother, and go into the land of Israel: for they are dead which sought the young child's life. And he arose, and took the young child and his mother, and came into the land of Israel. But when he heard that Archelaus did reign in Judaea in the room of his father Herod, he was afraid to go thither: notwithstanding, being warned of God in a dream, he turned aside into the parts of Galilee: And he came and dwelt in a city called Nazareth: that it might be fulfilled which was spoken by the prophets, He shall be called a Nazarene. (Matthew 2:19–23)

Joseph was diligent and discerning. The Lord told him to go to Israel, but he did not blindly go. When he learned that Herod's son was ruling, he went to the Lord with his fears. He sought and found confirmation of where he and his family should dwell in the shelter and protection of God the Father.

My Son,

Joseph is a perfect example of how you should lead your life. My prayer is for you to be a righteous, thoughtful, attentive, obedient, diligent, and discerning protector. Do not walk in fear of making mistakes. If you seek Him, you will find Him. "My sheep hear my voice, and they follow me" (John 10:27). Listen for His voice. Pray for confirmation if you are unsure what to do. He knows both your heart and your motives. If both your heart and your motives are pure in His sight, His grace will be sufficient for you and your family. My precious son, I love you with all my heart. I pray that you will have joy and peace abundantly throughout your life.

One more thing: Joseph did not seek to proclaim his rightness in the situation. He did not want to make sure that everyone knew that he was not the one who had impregnated Mary. He did not seek his own vindication. He knew who he was in the sight of the Lord, and that alone was all that he needed.

Be a Joseph.

CHAPTER 6

Marry a Mary

What is one word that describes Mary, the mother of Jesus? Mary was submissive.

Matthew 2

> And when they were departed, behold, the angel of the Lord appeareth to Joseph in a dream, saying, Arise, and take the young child and his mother, and flee into Egypt, and be thou there until I bring thee word: for Herod will seek the young child to destroy him. When he arose, he took the young

child and his mother by night, and departed into Egypt: And was there until the death of Herod: that it might be fulfilled which was spoken of the Lord by the prophet, saying, "Out of Egypt have I called my son." (Matthew 2:13–15)

When we read or listen to this passage, we may find it so familiar that we may not truly apply the example being displayed in Mary's character or see what the example of a submissive spirit she sets. She has traveled while pregnant on donkey back. She arrived at her destination only to find that there were no vacancies. She gave birth to this miraculous child. She was visited by the Magi. The child was very young. She was getting much-needed rest, and then she was awakened by her husband and was told that they must leave and go to another country.

It is not recorded that Mary questioned her husband. It may be assumed that she had learned "If the Lord is speaking to him, then He is speaking to me."

Luke 1

And in the sixth month the angel Gabriel was sent from God unto a city of Galilee, named Nazareth, To a virgin espoused to a man whose name was Joseph, of the house of David; and the virgin's name was Mary. And the angel came in unto her, and said, Hail, thou that art highly favoured, the Lord is with thee: blessed art thou among women. And when she saw him, she was troubled at his saying, and cast in her mind what manner of salutation this should be. (Luke 1:26–29)

We see in verse 29 that Mary was troubled. She was fearful. But even with her troubled and fearful spirit, she listened to God's message to her. God has a message for us also, which is the Holy Word of God that tells us that He loved us before we loved Him. He sent His one and only begotten Son for us. The penalty for our sin is already paid. He has a plan and purpose for us. If we delight ourselves in Him, then He will guard our path.

> And the angel said unto her, Fear not, Mary: for thou hast found favour with God. And, behold, thou shalt conceive in thy womb, and bring forth a son, and shalt call his name Jesus. He shall be great, and shall be called the Son of the Highest: and the Lord God shall give unto him the throne of his father David: And he shall reign over the house of Jacob for ever; and of his kingdom there shall be no end. Then said Mary unto the angel, How shall this be, seeing I know not a man? (Luke 1:30–34)

In verse 34, Mary questioned how it was possible that she was to conceive a child. We can empathize with her questioning and imagine her thought processes. I would venture to say that she saw the situation for what it was as an earthly situation and wondered how it was humanly impossible. She looked at her earthly condition, how things had always been, how she had always seen them, how things had happened before, and how these things were judged and looked upon by others, along with the expected outcome of what was to come. This questioning is understandable. We immediately question with the same thought processes in our everyday lives.

> And the angel answered and said unto her, The Holy Ghost shall come upon thee, and the power of the Highest shall overshadow thee: therefore also that holy thing which shall be born of thee

> shall be called the Son of God. And, behold, thy
> cousin Elisabeth, she hath also conceived a son
> in her old age: and this is the sixth month with
> her, who was called barren. For with God nothing
> shall be impossible. (Luke 1:35–37)

Her response to the angel's reply to her question reflects an exceptional quality indeed. The following scripture describes how Mary responded after she'd heard the angel say, "For nothing is impossible with God":

> Behold the handmaid of the Lord; be it unto me
> according to thy word. And the angel departed
> from her. (Luke 1:38)

In *faithful*, submitted meekness, Mary replied, "Be it unto me according to thy word" (Luke 1:38). Her response was *meek*. The true definition of meekness is the ability to serve without resentment.

She was *content* to serve in the role in which she was placed. This role was an *unexpected role*. She did not have a moment to prepare.

This role *redefined her position* within her community. She would undoubtedly be subject to ridicule and scrutiny, but her trust in the One who called her to this role was something she did not question. She *did not question* how this pregnancy would affect her life, but she submitted to the role she was placed in. She didn't look back and say, "But I have been a faithful young lady! Why do I have to endure this?" She didn't look at her current position and doubt—*I am engaged to be married. What will happen now?*

No. She did question the human impossibilities, but once she received her answer, *she believed, she trusted,* and she hoped for good, not evil.

And Mary arose in those days, and went into the hill country with haste, into a city of Juda; And entered into the house of Zacharias, and saluted Elisabeth. And it came to pass, that, when Elisabeth heard the salutation of Mary, the babe leaped in her womb; and Elisabeth was filled with the Holy Ghost: And she spake out with a loud voice, and said, Blessed art thou among women, and blessed is the fruit of thy womb. And whence is this to me, that the mother of my Lord should come to me? For, lo, as soon as the voice of thy salutation sounded in mine ears, the babe leaped in my womb for joy. And blessed is she that believed: for there shall be a performance of those things which were told her from the Lord. (Luke 1:39–45)

As Elizabeth stated, "And blessed is she that believed: for there shall be a performance of those things which were told her from the Lord" (Luke 1:45).

What was Mary's response to this?

And Mary said, My soul doth magnify the Lord, And my spirit hath rejoiced in God my Saviour. For he hath regarded the low estate of his handmaiden: for, behold, from henceforth all generations shall call me blessed. For he that is mighty hath done to me great things; and holy is his name. And his mercy is on them that fear him from generation to generation. He hath shewed strength with his arm; he hath scattered the proud in the imagination of their hearts. He hath put down the mighty from their seats, and exalted them of low degree. He

hath filled the hungry with good things; and the
rich he hath sent empty away. He hath helped
his servant Israel, in remembrance of his mercy.
(Luke 1:46–54)

Mary gave God glory. She recounted His faithfulness. She was thankful.

Thankful for what? Thankful for this new role in her life? Thankful for the paradigm shift in her life? Thankful for having been selected to bear this child? Yes, she was thankful. She considered it pure joy to endure this trial. She testified of His faithfulness and proclaimed the works He had already done. She recalled His mercies and His justices. She spoke His Word and recounted His promises.

What an example we have set before us to show us how to respond to change, whether good or bad. By the way, this is a great example of why we should journal our prayer requests and His answers to our requests. Not only do these journals serve to encourage us and remind us of His works, but also when we find ourselves in a situation that may require years of prayer and waiting for His answer, we can look to our journal to remember His faithfulness in the past and cling to His Word for our future.

Later in Luke, the shepherds came to see the baby and shared how the angels had appeared to them and greeted them in the same manner as they had greeted Mary, telling them not to be afraid. After the shepherds departed, the Bible tells us that everyone was amazed at what the shepherds had shared. "But Mary kept all these things, and pondered them in her heart" (Luke 2:19).

What did she ponder? Did she ponder what could have, should have, or would have been? Did she ponder, *If only this had happened?* Did she ponder, *If I would have just said this?*

No. She pondered all *things.*

I doubt that she ever looked back or pondered the what-ifs,

for she rested on His promises, His truths, and His Word spoken to her heart.

She pondered the promises spoken to her. She pondered the calling placed upon her. She pondered the imploring of the Lord, "Fear not" (Luke 1:30). She pondered, "I bring you good tidings of great joy, which shall be to all people" (Luke 2:10). She pondered how the Lord revealed Himself not only to her but also to others, and how they'd heard, "For unto you is born this day in the city of David a Saviour, which is Christ the Lord" (Luke 1:11). She pondered how they were told and shown where and when. She pondered how God is a God of specific detail. She pondered how the shepherds knew they would find a baby wrapped in cloths lying in a manger. She pondered how a great heavenly host appeared to them, saying, "Glory to God in the highest, and on earth peace, good will toward men" (Luke 2:14).

She treasured. She submitted. She meekly served without fear of harm.

There is so much we can learn from Mary. She believed what was told to her. In her Son's ministry, she submitted to Him. She released Him to be the man He was called to be. She did not try to defend His character when He was attacked. She did not try to fix things. She allowed God to do His work.

At His death she wept, but she did not cry out against the injustices being placed on her Son. No, she was submitting. She had the promises in her heart. She was meek. She was thankful and content. The only way to live through this beautiful responsibility placed upon her to mother this Holy Son of God was to store up all these treasures and ponder them in her heart.

My son, may you and your wife choose to treasure what the Lord has called you both to do each and every day without resentment, submitting to His allowances in your lives, relying on His promises, recalling His mercies, testifying of His power and love, being thankful for each and every day given, cherishing, treasuring, and pondering.

Mary was a human wife and mother. She questioned the human impossibilities, but she chose to believe in the Sovereign Lord. May you and your wife live out the following: "And make it your ambition to lead a quiet life: You should mind your own business and work with your hands, just as we told you so that your daily life may win the respect of outsiders and so that you will not be dependent on anybody" (1 Thessalonians 4:11). This is how Mary lived.

One last thing to consider: it is just as important to learn from what Mary possibly had to endure, which was criticism. Let's consider how others may have looked upon her. I feel sure that there were those who continued to doubt her character and doubt *that* carpenter she had married. Life is full of criticism. May you and your wife not waver in your callings on account of criticism. Know your calling. Stay determined to fulfill God's purposes for your life. Be a team. This is another reason why it is important to make sure your wife is a safe haven for you, someone with whom you can share your heart. May Mary's story also show you the importance of being careful not to judge others or to make assumptions without knowing the entire story. May we not display a critical spirit ourselves toward others.

> Let the words of my mouth, and the meditation of
> my heart, be acceptable in thy sight, O Lord, my
> strength, and my redeemer. (Psalm 19:14)

CHAPTER 7

Hosea

The word of the Lord that came unto Hosea, the son of Beeri, in the days of Uzziah, Jotham, Ahaz, and Hezekiah, kings of Judah, and in the days of Jeroboam the son of Joash, king of Israel. The beginning of the word of the Lord by Hosea. And the Lord said to Hosea, Go, take unto thee a wife of whoredoms and children of whoredoms: for the land hath committed great whoredom, departing from the Lord. So he went and took Gomer the daughter of Diblaim; which conceived, and bare him a son. —Hosea 1:1–3

When the Lord says to Hosea, "Go, take unto thee a wife of whoredoms" (Hosea 1:2), I cannot help but see the resemblance to a conversation between an earthly father and a son who refuses to heed his father's warnings. The father warned him about the sinful people and about the sin of the land, but the son refused to listen to or heed the warning. Finally, after the son continued to deceive himself into thinking that these warnings do not apply to him, or that these warnings of danger will not affect him. The father said, "Go ahead. Do what you want. You will have to learn the hard way since you will not heed. Marry into whoredom." We all have free will. The Lord will not make us be obedient. He wants us to love Him so much that we will want to please Him through our obedience. If we refuse to heed His warnings, He will allow us to go our own way and be married to our sins.

I pray that the Lord will be your guide and that you will seek confirmation from Him through the study of God's Word and the conviction of the Holy Spirit regarding your selection of a wife. As you see in Hosea, the Lord will *allow* you to marry an adulteress. He gives us free will. Gomer was not a harlot when Hosea married her, but God warned him that she would be unfaithful.[10] *It is important not to allow yourself an opportunity to give your heart away, not even in the slightest, to one who is unfaithful.* What does it mean not to allow opportunity? It means not to look upon things that are not pure, not to flirt with those who are flirtatious, not to befriend a girl before observing her ways. If you avoid doing these things, then you will not allow your heart to be turned to her, for once you begin to love her, your compassion and pardon for inexcusable behaviors will begin. Remember, love covers a multitude of sins (1 Peter 4:8). If you begin to love her, you will cover sins that otherwise would have served as a warning. Your protector instincts will want to rescue her from her life because God places in every

---

[10] Warren Wiersbe, *Bible Commentary: Old Testament* (Nashville: Thomas Nelson, 1991).

young man's heart the yearning to protect. *This yearning to protect will be spent in vain if the heart of the woman is not yours to protect.* Your love for her will cause you not to heed the warnings from those who love you.

Love is a deep and strong affection that will cause you to be willing to do almost anything for your loved ones. It is important to be with one who is grounded in God's Word. That way, the desire to protect and provide will be satisfied by the two of you being unified in the cause of Christ. A united home allows your energy and effort to be spent protecting your united hearts from Satan's attacks. Your energy and effort will not be spent going through a wilderness filled with deception and sin in your *own home* but on concentrating your efforts on the wilderness the Lord has for all His children, for we Christians are aliens in this world.

Hosea 2

> Therefore, behold, I will allure her, and bring her into the wilderness, and speak comfortably unto her. And I will give her her vineyards from thence, and the valley of Achor for a door of hope. (Hosea 2:14–15)

In this passage, Hosea is leading Gomer through the wilderness while fulfilling his duties as her husband. He is loving, nurturing, leading, guiding, and protecting her. His desire is to give her back what she has lost. He is a picture of God's grace in our sinful lives. Because he has an adulterous wife, he is trying to mend what is broken. *We all walk through the wilderness of this world. Whether you walk it alone or with one who is like-minded and unified in Christ makes all the difference in the world.* There is nothing lonelier in this life than to be a Christian living in a home not unified in Christ. As a provider, you will be in this world surrounded by people who are looking out for themselves. Being like-minded in your home allows you and your wife to work together as a team for a common purpose: walking through the wilderness together with you looking out for the traps of Satan in order to protect your wife and children. Not only will you heed what the Lord reveals to your heart, but also you will have a helpmeet who is listening to the Lord's direction for her life. And, honey, if God is speaking to her, then He is speaking to you. And if God is speaking to you, then He is speaking to her. You are one in God's sight. If your heart is entangled with an unbeliever, then not only will you face the wilderness in this world, but also you will face it in your home while trying to protect your spouse from herself, as well as trying to protect your own heart from being hurt.

Let's look at what Hosea endured:

> Plead with your mother, plead: for she is not my wife, neither am I her husband: let her therefore put away her whoredoms out of her sight, and her adulteries from between her breasts; Lest I strip her naked, and set her as in the day that she was born, and make her as a wilderness, and set her like a dry land, and slay her with thirst. And I will not have mercy upon her children; for they be the children of whoredoms. (Hosea 2:2–4)

Notice he has no joy in their children. They are not his to love, and even if they are, how can he be sure?

> For their mother hath played the harlot: she that conceived them hath done shamefully: for she said, I will go after my lovers, that give me my bread and my water, my wool and my flax, mine oil and my drink. Therefore, behold, I will hedge up thy way with thorns, and make a wall, that she shall not find her paths. And she shall follow

after her lovers, but she shall not overtake them; and she shall seek them, but shall not find them: then shall she say, I will go and return to my first husband; for then was it better with me than now. For she did not know that I gave her corn, and wine, and oil, and multiplied her silver and gold, which they prepared for Baal. (Hosea 2:5–8)

Not one thing he has done for her has been appreciated, nor was it "enough."

Therefore will I return, and take away my corn in the time thereof, and my wine in the season thereof, and will recover my wool and my flax given to cover her nakedness. And now will I discover her lewdness in the sight of her lovers, and none shall deliver her out of mine hand. (Hosea 2:9–10)

His heart is filled with vengeance. He wants to make it so that no one will want his wife.

And I will destroy her vines and her fig trees, whereof she hath said, "These are my rewards that my lovers have given me: and I will make them a forest, and the beasts of the field shall eat them." And I will visit upon her the days of Baalim, wherein she burned incense to them, and she decked herself with her earrings and her jewels, and she went after her lovers, and forgat me, saith the Lord. (Hosea 2:12–13)

Even in the face of consequence, she decks herself with adornment to pursue her lovers.

Now let's go back to verses 14 and 15:

Therefore, behold, I will allure her, and bring her into the wilderness, and speak comfortably unto her. And I will give her her vineyards from thence, and the valley of Achor for a door of hope: and she shall sing there, as in the days of her youth, and as in the day when she came up out of the land of Egypt. (Hosea 2:14–15)

This takes place after he has withstood all those things. He is leading her back to her vineyards and back to his love and care. What a picture of grace! It is beautiful, yes! But it is *hard*. It is a hard road that requires devotion to the Lord that is greater than the hurt Hosea experienced through his wife's unfaithfulness. Yes, you can endure this kind of life, but this is *not* the life the Lord wants for you. Nor do I think He wanted it for Hosea. Yet He allowed it. And He will allow it in your life if you are not willing to heed His warnings.

The Lord does not want any of us to spend all our efforts to win a heart that was never ours to love. No, the Lord wants us to be in a blessed marriage so that we will be able to safely trust in our spouse, which will allow us to be more productive for His kingdom.

Hosea 3

Then said the Lord unto me, Go yet, love a woman beloved of her friend, yet an adulteress, according to the love of the Lord toward the children of Israel, who look to other gods, and love flagons of wine. So I bought her to me for fifteen pieces of silver, and for an homer of barley, and an half homer of barley: And I said unto her, Thou shalt abide for me many days; thou shalt not play the harlot, and thou shalt not be for another man: so will I also be for thee. (Hosea 3:1–3)

The book of Hosea is such a beautiful picture of a husband's love for his wife—a husband willing to go through the wilderness of life with her. In the wilderness, one faces many dangers. You are susceptible to predators that sneak up on you like a roaring lion. You are alone. There are very few of like mind in the wilderness. Savages are there. These savages work by instinct alone with no compassion for others. The food and water are only for those who know their way through the wilderness. It is for those who have walked that trail before and for those who have learned the ways of the wilderness. In the wilderness, savages are considered wise, yet the place is filled with echoes of loneliness. Life in the wilderness is a picture of this world we live in.

As the provider for your home, you will be forced to work and live the majority of your days in the wilderness. Marriage is a picture of God's love providing all that you need for survival in the wilderness. It should be a safe haven from the wilderness, a place where you come to rest with your helpmeet, being understood, loved, and safe. Marriage is a picture of the Lord and His bride. This relationship should serve to provide you with the spiritual encouragement to face the dangers in the wilderness each day. The wilderness is not nearly as lonely when you have someone beside you who loves you, someone who looks out for your best interests, someone who wants what is best for you. In the wilderness, the forest is filled with those who only look out for themselves. They don't care about what is best for anyone except themselves. There are those who take advantage during loss. You may think that these savages are easily identifiable, but, honey, they mask themselves well. They portray themselves to be one thing, but in their heart they are another.

Son, my prayer is that you will not have to walk through this life lonely. You may be surrounded by people but still be very lonely. I pray that you seek a wife who will provide you with the love and encouragement you need in order to face this world head-on each day with godly character and integrity. I pray that you will be able to face each day knowing that when you get home, you will find rest.

"And Isaac brought her into his mother Sarah's tent, and took Rebekah, and she became his wife; and he loved her: and Isaac was comforted after his mother's death. Isaac was comforted by Rebekah after the passing of his mother" (Genesis 24:67). No one will love you like your mother. The love of a mother for her child is like no other, but once your heart has joined with your wife in marriage, you will experience the love of a beautifully nurturing, sweet-spirited wife, which is the next love that is like no other. My son, when I pass from this world, I want to have the comfort of knowing that you will be comforted by an unselfish, trustworthy, sacrificially loving wife. I want to know that she will comfort you to the best of her ability, love you, and care for you during your loss and take care of you when I am no longer able. This is my prayer. I pray that you will have a bond with her like no other.

CHAPTER 8

Hannah

1 Samuel 1

Now there was a certain man of Ramathaimzophim, of mount Ephraim, and his name was Elkanah, the son of Jeroham, the son of Elihu, the son of Tohu, the son of Zuph, an Ephrathite: And he had two wives; the name of the one was Hannah, and the name of the other Peninnah: and Peninnah

had children, but Hannah had no children. And
this man went up out of his city yearly to worship
and to sacrifice unto the Lord of hosts in Shiloh.
And the two sons of Eli, Hophni and Phinehas,
the priests of the Lord, were there. And when
the time was that Elkanah offered, he gave to
Peninnah his wife, and to all her sons and her
daughters, portions: But unto Hannah he gave a
worthy portion; for he loved Hannah: but the Lord
had shut up her womb. And her adversary also
provoked her sore, for to make her fret, because
the Lord had shut up her womb. And as he did
so year by year, when she went up to the house of
the Lord, so she provoked her; therefore she wept,
and did not eat. Then said Elkanah her husband
to her, Hannah, why weepest thou? and why eatest
thou not? and why is thy heart grieved? am not I
better to thee than ten sons? (1 Samuel 1:1–8)

One of Hannah's characteristics that stands out to me is her
perseverance. She continues to seek the Lord year after year in
the hope that He will fulfill the desires of her heart. You can
imagine how year after year she must have walked away from the
house of the Lord, hoping that this would be the year she would
bear a child. Year after year, she went to worship even though the
previous year she still had not received the desire of her heart. She
continued to go worship and to lay her requests before the Lord
even though she had wept and petitioned the Lord to no avail
in years past. She took the trip to worship Him and to offer Him
sacrifices. She did not become defeated by her mistreatment. She
did not give up on petitioning the Lord for the desire of her heart.

So Hannah rose up after they had eaten in Shiloh,
and after they had drunk. Now Eli the priest sat

upon a seat by a post of the temple of the Lord. And she was in bitterness of soul, and prayed unto the Lord, and wept sore. And she vowed a vow, and said, O Lord of hosts, if thou wilt indeed look on the affliction of thine handmaid, and remember me, and not forget thine handmaid, but wilt give unto thine handmaid a man child, then I will give him unto the Lord all the days of his life, and there shall no razor come upon his head. (1 Samuel 1:9–11)

There may be an inclination in her prayer that she felt forgotten by the Lord, but that did not stop her from laying her requests at His feet. That is true faith, to feel forgotten yet still recognize that He is there, and to feel unheard yet still believe that He is sovereign in all He does. She continued to gently and respectfully plead with Him, asking that He fulfill the desires of her heart. She persevered. She was not frustrated and did not turn away from her faith, saying, "There must be no God, for He has not answered." No, she endured with an undying faith in Him, recognizing He had not given her the desires of her heart and continually sharing with Him her hurts. She waited in expectancy.

My son, this quality of steadfast faith and perseverance amid extreme trials is a quality to be desired in a wife. Life brings trials that do not make sense. When all feels lost, you want to be able to cling to someone who will continue to plead with the Lord for the desires of your hearts.

And it came to pass, as she continued praying before the Lord, that Eli marked her mouth. Now Hannah, she spake in her heart; only her lips moved, but her voice was not heard: therefore Eli thought she had been drunken. And Eli said unto her, How long wilt thou be drunken? put away thy wine from thee. (1 Samuel 1:12–14)

After pouring her heart out to the Lord, asking Him not to forget his servant and pleading to Him, "Remember me," Hannah was interrupted by the priest Eli, who accused her of being drunk. That would have been enough for most people to turn away from the Lord. I can imagine most of our responses would involve asking, "What? Why? Why, Lord, would You have this priest ask me if I am drunk? This is supposed to be a place of prayer, a place where I am to lay my requests out before You. I have come here pleading for the desires of my heart. Not only have I been subject to mistreatment by the one who bore my husband's children as she has held this over me day after day, year after year, but also while I am laying my requests before You, You allow this person of faith to accuse me of something I have not done. Why, Lord?" But, praise the Lord, this is *not* the response we see from Hannah.

> And Hannah answered and said, No, my lord, I am
> a woman of a sorrowful spirit: I have drunk neither
> wine nor strong drink, but have poured out my
> soul before the Lord. Count not thine handmaid
> for a daughter of Belial: for out of the abundance
> of my complaint and grief have I spoken hitherto.
> (1 Samuel 1:15–16)

What a remarkably beautiful response from Hannah, one that we should apply to our own lives. She did not fall into a greater depression or completely cry out in despair over the injustices being done against her. She humbly responded, "No, my Lord."

"No, my Lord"? Wow! She continued to recognize the Lord's sovereignty. She respectfully honored the one the Lord has put in place to serve Him. She knew that the Lord allowed Eli to be there, that he was placed there to witness her prayer, and that he was allowed to surround her with these accusations. I believe that because of her humility and submission to his ordained authority, because she did not turn away in bitterness, and because she continued in her commitment to wait on the Lord, the Lord allowed Eli's response to her to be one of grace.

> Then Eli answered and said, Go in peace: and the God of Israel grant thee thy petition that thou hast asked of him (1 Samuel 1:17).

She left hopeful. Hannah did not victimize herself. She continuously went to the Lord, waiting in expectancy. "The effectual fervent prayer of a righteous man availeth much" (James 5:16b). She was strong in her faith. Sometimes our circumstances are not for us but for others. Eli's accusation was not meant for Hannah's defeat. I believe it was meant for Eli to witness a deeply troubled lady praying out in anguish and grief. Eli needed to know the faithful, earnest pleas of Hannah's heart in order to accept Samuel as the Lord's appointed. The Lord gave Hannah the desire to have children. He placed that desire within her heart. It was a longing that she had to endure. It was also a longing that in Peninnah's eyes was a source of weakness, which she found to be a useful tool to use against Hannah on a daily basis. *All of these so-called "defeats" did not snuff out Hannah's faith. Instead they strengthened it. God knew that for her to be able to give her child over to Him, it would require a faith and strength that could only come from a heart completely devoted to His sovereignty.*

My son, you must look for a lady to be strong in her faith, not one to bow down to others, not one to bow down to her circumstances, and not one caught up in the trap of comparing herself to others. Instead seek a lady who looks up only to Him, knowing His sovereignty is sufficient for all her needs. In this life, attacks come. Things don't make sense at times. The timing of things, from our viewpoint, may be at its worst. May you seek a wife who will patiently wait on the Lord, one who will peacefully rest in the fact that His ways are not our ways and His timing is not our timing. Hannah was a lady of her word. She was faithful and obedient. She did not bargain with the Lord for Samuel but rather was completely devoted to the Lord, wanting to honor Him with the gift of her heart's desire.

A lady must be willing to obey even when it hurts beyond all measure. Can you imagine Hannah's long walk home after giving her child to Eli? Yet she came home, dying to self and continuing to hope in Him. She made a robe for Samuel each year. I believe this robe is a symbol of hope in our Lord. She had to have made each robe every year with the expectation that he had grown in that year, not only in stature but also in the Lord. Making this robe each year is a lesson for us to keep on keeping on even while we are waiting for Him to fulfill His purposes. We must not wallow in our heartache of loss—in Hannah's case, the loss of a child in her care—but must remember what He has called us to do, remember what we dedicated and committed to Him, and continue to be faithful and to serve Him, waiting in expectancy.

> And she said, Let thine handmaid find grace in thy sight. So the woman went her way, and did eat, and her countenance was no more sad. And they rose up in the morning early, and worshipped before the Lord, and returned, and came to their house to Ramah: and Elkanah knew Hannah his wife; and the Lord remembered her. Wherefore it came to pass, when the time was come about after Hannah had conceived, that she bare a son, and called his name Samuel, saying, Because I have asked him of the Lord. And the man Elkanah, and all his house, went up to offer unto the Lord the yearly sacrifice, and his vow. But Hannah went not up; for she said unto her husband, I will not go up until the child be weaned, and then I will bring him, that he may appear before the Lord, and there abide for ever. And Elkanah her

husband said unto her, Do what seemeth thee good; tarry until thou have weaned him; only the Lord establish his word. So the woman abode, and gave her son suck until she weaned him. And when she had weaned him, she took him up with her, with three bullocks, and one ephah of flour, and a bottle of wine, and brought him unto the house of the Lord in Shiloh: and the child was young. And they slew a bullock, and brought the child to Eli. And she said, Oh my lord, as thy soul liveth, my lord, I am the woman that stood by thee here, praying unto the Lord. For this child I prayed; and the Lord hath given me my petition which I asked of him: Therefore also I have lent him to the Lord; as long as he liveth he shall be lent to the Lord. And he worshipped the Lord there. (1 Samuel 1:18–28)

1 Samuel 2

And Hannah prayed, and said, My heart rejoiceth in the Lord, mine horn is exalted in the Lord: my mouth is enlarged over mine enemies; because I rejoice in thy salvation. There is none holy as the Lord: for there is none beside thee: neither is there any rock like our God. Talk no more so exceeding proudly; let not arrogancy come out of your mouth: for the Lord is a God of knowledge, and by him actions are weighed. The bows of the mighty men are broken, and they that stumbled are girded with strength. They that were full have hired out themselves for bread; and they that were hungry ceased: so that the barren hath born seven; and she that hath many children is waxed feeble.

The Lord killeth, and maketh alive: he bringeth down to the grave, and bringeth up. The Lord maketh poor, and maketh rich: he bringeth low, and lifteth up. He raiseth up the poor out of the dust, and lifteth up the beggar from the dunghill, to set them among princes, and to make them inherit the throne of glory: for the pillars of the earth are the Lord's, and he hath set the world upon them. He will keep the feet of his saints, and the wicked shall be silent in darkness; for by strength shall no man prevail. The adversaries of the Lord shall be broken to pieces; out of heaven shall he thunder upon them: the Lord shall judge the ends of the earth; and he shall give strength unto his king, and exalt the horn of his anointed. And Elkanah went to Ramah to his house. And the child did minister unto the Lord before Eli the priest. Now the sons of Eli were sons of Belial; they knew not the Lord. And the priest's custom with the people was, that, when any man offered sacrifice, the priest's servant came, while the flesh was in seething, with a fleshhook of three teeth in his hand; And he struck it into the pan, or kettle, or caldron, or pot; all that the fleshhook brought up the priest took for himself. So they did in Shiloh unto all the Israelites that came thither. Also before they burnt the fat, the priest's servant came, and said to the man that sacrificed, Give flesh to roast for the priest; for he will not have sodden flesh of thee, but raw. And if any man said unto him, Let them not fail to burn the fat presently, and then take as much as thy soul desireth; then he would answer him, Nay; but thou shalt give it me now: and if not, I will take it by force. Wherefore the sin of the young men was very great before the Lord: for men abhorred the offering of the Lord. (1 Samuel 2:1–17)

Hannah's hope was in none other than the Lord, for she must have known Eli's sons were evil. Yet she did not try to micromanage and look for another tabernacle with a better, godlier priest who had done a better job of raising his sons. She did not say, "Lord, I know that I told You that if you gave me a son, I would give him to You, but, Lord, this man is not even a good father to his own children. I must find a more suitable place. Surely You didn't call me to give my son over to him. There must be another priest who will do a better job." No, she fully trusted in the Lord, not man, recognizing that His ways are not our ways. She completely trusted in Him even when the circumstances were not perfect. Mankind will always disappoint us, but God never will.

But Samuel ministered before the Lord, being a child, girded with a linen ephod. Moreover his mother made him a little coat, and brought it to him from year to year, when she came up with her husband to offer the yearly sacrifice. And Eli blessed Elkanah and his wife, and said, The Lord give thee seed of this woman for the loan which is lent to the Lord. And they went unto their own home. And the Lord visited Hannah, so that she conceived, and bare three sons and two daughters. And the child Samuel grew before the Lord. (2 Samuel 2:18–21)

The Lord blessed Hannah for her faithfulness. She not only was given the honor to love, nurture, and raise five more children, but she also had a peace beyond all understanding in the fact that Samuel grew up in the protection of the Lord.

My Son,

Hannah is a picture of pure beauty, love, and undying devotion to the Lord. She truly is a picture of the wife I envision for you. I pray not only that you will find a wife with that kind of devotion but also that you will be that kind of husband to her, one who is faithful no matter the circumstances, believing in Him and relying on Him to fulfill His purposes and promises. I pray that you will be one who continues to plead with the Lord for the desires of your heart no matter the circumstances or how long it takes. I pray you will point your wife to the Lord when her faith falters and that she will do the same for you when yours falters. Be steadfast. Be strong in the Lord. Be honoring. Be faithful. Trust.

CHAPTER 9

Peter

Son, the Lord has placed on my heart to share an encouragement with you that He has given to me. This is something that He has taught me that I have had to take to heart and take to the Cross. I hope that this encourages you too.

Let's think about the disciples for a moment. These men

basically lived with Jesus for three years. They ate together, listened to his teachings, and ministered together.

The following passage from the book of Mark takes place just after Jesus and His disciples had partaken in the Lord's Supper together:

> And when they had sung an hymn, they went out into the mount of Olives. And Jesus saith unto them, All ye shall be offended because of me this night: for it is written, I will smite the shepherd, and the sheep shall be scattered. But after that I am risen, I will go before you into Galilee. But Peter said unto him, Although all shall be offended, yet will not I. And Jesus saith unto him, Verily I say unto thee, That this day, even in this night, before the cock crow twice, thou shalt deny me thrice. But he spake the more vehemently, If I should die with thee, I will not deny thee in any wise. Likewise also said they all. And they came to a place which was named Gethsemane: and he saith to his disciples, Sit ye here, while I shall pray. And he taketh with him Peter and James and John, and began to be sore amazed, and to be very heavy; And saith unto them, My soul is exceeding sorrowful unto death: tarry ye here, and watch. And he went forward a little, and fell on the ground, and prayed that, if it were possible, the hour might pass from him. And he said, Abba, Father, all things are possible unto thee; take away this cup from me: nevertheless not what I will, but what thou wilt. And he cometh, and findeth them sleeping, and saith unto Peter, Simon, sleepest thou? couldest not thou watch one hour? Watch ye and pray, lest ye enter into

temptation. The spirit truly is ready, but the flesh
is weak. (Mark 14:26–38)

Here, we see that Jesus recognized and announced that they would
all fall away. The disciples, His dearest and closest friends here
on earth, are the ones into whom He had poured Himself day
after day. They are the ones He had prayed with and shared His
future with. He taught them daily, fully expecting that after they
had been taught, they would apply those teachings to their own
lives, and then go and make disciples of others. Yet He knew that
they would all fall away, even Peter. Peter, the one who showed
the most heartfelt devotion to the Lord, claimed emphatically, "I
will die with you if I have to." Even he fell asleep while the Lord
was praying.

Once Jesus was taken away from them, the disciples faced
a crisis of belief, a true crisis of faith: *they needed to decide for
themselves, "Whom shall I serve?"* Not one of them immediately
chose whom they would serve. Not one said, "As for me and my
house, we will serve the Lord" (Joshua 24:15). No, actually quite
the opposite occurred. Just as Jesus had spoken, they all fell away.

John 18

And Simon Peter followed Jesus, and so did
another disciple: that disciple was known unto
the high priest, and went in with Jesus into the
palace of the high priest. But Peter stood at the
door without. Then went out that other disciple,
which was known unto the high priest, and spake
unto her that kept the door, and brought in Peter.
Then saith the damsel that kept the door unto
Peter, Art not thou also one of this man's disciples?
He saith, I am not. And the servants and officers
stood there, who had made a fire of coals; for it

was cold: and they warmed themselves: and Peter stood with them, and warmed himself. The high priest then asked Jesus of his disciples, and of his doctrine. Jesus answered him, I spake openly to the world; I ever taught in the synagogue, and in the temple, whither the Jews always resort; and in secret have I said nothing. Why askest thou me? ask them which heard me, what I have said unto them: behold, they know what I said. And when he had thus spoken, one of the officers which stood by struck Jesus with the palm of his hand, saying, Answerest thou the high priest so? Jesus answered him, If I have spoken evil, bear witness of the evil: but if well, why smitest thou me? Now Annas had sent him bound unto Caiaphas the high priest. And Simon Peter stood and warmed himself. They said therefore unto him, Art not thou also one of his disciples? He denied it, and said, I am not. One of the servants of the high priest, being his kinsman whose ear Peter cut off, saith, Did not I see thee in the garden with him? Peter then denied again: and immediately the cock crew. (John 18:15–27)

I am focusing on Peter because the Lord focused on Peter. I believe the Lord gives us the specific details regarding Peter's betrayal and the specific details regarding the Lord's charge to Peter to feed His sheep to serve as an encouragement to us. *The betrayals that hurt the most come from those we least expect it from.* When we experience any form of rebellion or betrayal from trusted family members or dear friends, it is a pain like no other, especially when we have poured our hearts and lives into them. We have given of our time and our love and have truly invested in the relationship. We may have taught them the truths of God's Word, or we may have shared experiences in studying God's Word together. We tend to believe that these relationships will *never* let us down because they are built on Christian values.

Have we placed an expectation on our circumstances that exalts itself higher than the Lord's circumstances? Do we expect something more from our trusted relationships than what the Lord Himself experienced with His disciples?

I'm not saying that we should never trust, but we need always to be praying for protection in our relationships and pray for the hearts of those we hold dear. *Man will let us down, but the Lord never will.*

The Lord blesses us with such an encouragement through this teaching about Peter.

Peter comes into his own.

Peter comes to his *own* faith apart from Jesus.

Peter is a classic example of a child's rebellious spirit or a loved one's betrayal.

Jesus foretold what was going to happen. He warned Peter. But Peter did not want to hear it, nor did he want to believe it.

Peter was too confident in his faith outside of Jesus, outside of Jesus's strength, and outside of Jesus's leadership in his life. *Once Peter was alone and separated from Jesus's leadership, his weaknesses were exposed through his denial.* The realization of how easily he'd been persuaded to conform to the world around him pierced his heart. He realized that he was capable of denying the Lord and that he was truly hiding from his identity in Christ. He wanted to blend in with the crowd.

It was the convicting power of the Lord Jesus, through the rooster crowing, that brought about the realization of the truth of Jesus's words, which came to life and pierced Peter's heart. He knew he had to make a decision, and he knew that it was his choice as to whom he would serve. He had to answer the questions "Is my faith only true when I'm with the one who leads me, the one who teaches me, the one who disciples me, the one I have lived with and followed for years? Am I going to choose to be identified as a follower of Christ? Will I remain in fellowship with other believers? Will I use and apply the wisdom that has been poured into me? Will I apply the Word of the Lord that has transformed my life, and use these things to lead others to a saving knowledge of the Lord's sacrificial love for them?" This was a crisis of belief. We all go through a crisis of belief at some time or another. Some of us may ask these questions when we face hardships that seem too hard to bear or when things just don't make sense. Some of us ask these questions when we are no longer under our parental authority. No matter the circumstance, we all must decide whom we are going to serve and honor, and ultimately with whom we will be identified.

John 21

After these things Jesus shewed himself again to the disciples at the sea of Tiberias; and on this wise shewed he himself. There were together Simon Peter, and Thomas called Didymus, and Nathanael of Cana in Galilee, and the sons of Zebedee, and two other of his disciples. Simon Peter saith unto them, I go a fishing. They say unto him, We also go with thee. They went forth, and entered into a ship immediately; and that night they caught nothing. But when the morning was now come, Jesus stood on the shore: but the disciples knew not that it was Jesus. Then Jesus saith unto them, Children, have ye any meat? They answered him, No. And he said unto them, Cast the net on the right side of the ship, and ye shall find. They cast therefore, and now they were not able to draw it for the multitude of fishes. Therefore that disciple whom Jesus loved saith unto Peter, It is the Lord. Now when Simon Peter heard that it was the Lord, he girt his fisher's coat unto him, (for he was naked,) and did cast himself into the sea. And the other disciples came in a little ship; (for they were not far from land, but as it were two hundred cubits,) dragging the net with fishes. As soon then as they were come to land, they saw a fire of coals there, and fish laid thereon, and bread. Jesus saith unto them, Bring of the fish which ye have now caught. Simon Peter went up, and drew the net to land full of great fishes, an hundred and fifty and three: and for all there were so many, yet was not the net broken. Jesus saith unto them, Come and dine. And none of the disciples durst ask him, Who art thou? knowing that it was the Lord. Jesus then cometh, and taketh bread, and giveth them, and fish likewise. This is now the third time that Jesus shewed himself to his disciples, after that he was risen from the dead. So when they had dined, Jesus saith to Simon Peter, Simon, son of Jonas, lovest thou me more than these? He saith unto him, Yea, Lord; thou knowest that I love thee. He saith unto him, Feed my lambs. He saith to him again the second time, Simon, son of Jonas, lovest thou me? He saith unto him, Yea, Lord; thou knowest that I love thee. He saith unto him, Feed my sheep. He saith unto him the third time, Simon, son of Jonas, lovest thou me? Peter was grieved because he said unto him the third time, Lovest thou me? And he said unto him, Lord, thou knowest all things; thou knowest that I love thee. Jesus saith unto him, Feed my sheep. (John 21:1–17)

Jesus met the disciples in the same place He had met them before they chose to follow Him. We read how they were doing exactly what they were doing when they first encountered the Lord. They were fishing, just like before, and were not catching anything. Jesus called to them and told them where to put their nets in order to find fish.

When we see those we love running from the Lord and not living out what they have been taught, we must follow Jesus's example and lovingly meet them where they are. We must continue to point them in the right direction, toward the place where they will find success.

When Peter recognized the Lord, what did he do? He jumped into the water! I can't help but see his lack of self-control and self-discipline. This passion is the same passion that prompted him to declare his loyalty to the Lord, to proclaim that he would die for the Lord, and it is the same passion that caused him to refuse to believe that he was capable of denying the Lord. His lack of self-control and self-discipline prompted him to want to blend in, to not be willing to be ostracized, and to not be willing to stand up and be different. You see, passion does not equate to loyalty. *Passion, like feelings, can change based on your circumstances. Passion must be coupled with discipline and control.* Passion must be directed toward a cause greater than yourself. There will be Peters in your life, and believe it or not, you may even find yourself being a Peter at some points in your life.

> Jesus lovingly asked Peter, "Lovest thou me more than these?" He saith unto him, "Yea, Lord; thou knowest that I love thee." (John 21:15)

Did Peter truly mean it when he said that he loved the Lord, even though he denied Him? Yes. Yes, he did. He actually loved the Lord even when he denied Him, but he had to make a choice. He had to make the choice to sacrificially love. Loving someone does not mean only loving when the loved one is pouring into you. Loving does not mean only loving when the other is giving of his or her time and energy to you. No, that is a love that loves the benefits of the relationship. Loving what someone does for you or what you are receiving from the relationship is not complete and true love. True love is this: "that a man lay down his life for his friends" (John 15:13). Actions of true love are evident when a relationship has met a need in your life, and you continue to be loyal and nurture that relationship long after that need has been met. A perfect example is "hell insurance." When a person becomes saved and they know that their sins have been forgiven, they trust that they are going to heaven upon their death. Once they have received the "benefit" of Christ, they must decide if they are willing to live being identified with Christ. True love is not a selfish love. It is a serving love.

Three times the Lord told Peter:

Feed My lambs. Take care of My sheep. Feed My sheep.

The Lord's mercy was evident. Despite the mistakes Peter made, despite the sins he committed, including his denial of the Lord and his attempt to blend in with the world, the Lord had a mighty work for Peter.

Once Peter decided for himself to "choose you this day whom ye will serve" (Joshua 24:15), he then answered for himself: "But as for me and my house, we will serve the Lord" (Joshua 24:15).

The Lord did mighty things.

This encourages my heart so much. I wanted to share this with you because no matter what we have dedicated, no matter how much we have prayed, no matter how much love we have given, it is not more than what the Lord has already done for us. Trials will come so that He and He alone will get the glory. This is not to say that He does not bless what we have dedicated to Him, because, yes, He does bless our commitments to Him immensely. But we should not expect that there will be no trials and/or betrayals along the way. My prayer, my son, is that if you find yourself disappointed in others or disappointed in yourself, you won't give up. Peter disappointed himself, and he betrayed our Lord. It was no surprise to the Lord, and He used this betrayal to strengthen Peter's dependence on Him. Our hope and strength are found in the Lord alone. My prayer is that if you identify with Peter, you will choose you this day whom you will serve, and you will decide to serve the Lord with all your heart, soul, mind, and strength. If you find yourself betrayed by a trusted family member or friend, please know that the Lord is in such matters too. He is growing you to rely on Him and Him alone. He is also growing those who have betrayed you. Pray for them. Lay your burdens at the foot of the cross. Be sensitive to what the Lord is calling you to do, but also be careful and allow the Lord to do His work through His convicting power, which only He can give.

I love you, my precious son. May the Lord fill your heart with His peace, love, and rest.

CHAPTER 10

Identity Theft

What is your identity? If you were being interviewed and asked the following questions, how would you describe yourself? "Who are you? How do you see yourself? How do others see you? How does God see you and identify you?"

My favorite quote is by Dr. Charles Stanley. He says, "There are three people sitting in your seat today. There is the person that you think yourself to be. There is the person that others believe you to be. And, there is the person that God knows you to be."[11]

---

[11] Charles Stanley, pastor of First Baptist Church of Atlanta, ww.fba.org.

Satan wants to destroy your identity. He knows that if he can get you to doubt yourself to a great degree, then you will no longer feel equipped to fulfill the calling God has placed upon your life. You will not have the confidence to fulfill His purposes.

What is your identity wrapped up in? As you are growing into an adult and seeking the plan God has for your life, you may place your trust in the Lord to bless your efforts. You are hopeful in the plan that the Lord has called you to carry out. You cling to the promises in His Word. You are confident that certain actions will produce certain results. But what happens when things don't go as planned? What happens when the days are not the way you envisioned them to be? Satan will use those difficulties and perceived failures in your life to destroy your identity. I ask you, is your identity wrapped up in your successes? This is an extremely important question for every young man to ponder. The Lord calls every man to work, to provide, to protect, and to love. With so many tangible callings upon your life, it is easy to equate the tangible outcome with success in life. You work hard + You make good money = You buy a nice house.

When you experience a hardship or a struggle, or you encounter failure, what becomes of your identity then? Are you a failure? a doubter? a falterer? broken? If the economy takes a hit, your job is eliminated, and you lose your home, are you now a failure? If having a nice house equals success in your eyes, then if you lose your home, will the opposite be true? No. But Satan would definitely have you believe these things, wouldn't he? Believing that if we do this, it will automatically produce that is a lie. He wants us to believe that if we do this and don't get that, then we must be failing. How Satan must be enjoying the fact that we wrap our identities around the evidence or products of success in our lives.

Trials are necessary. They are needful for our faith. Trials are not our identity.

So in the end, what is our identity? Is our identity wrapped up in our success or the success of those around us? No. This attitude of so-called success is a trap brought about by our tendency to compare our success with another's success, and the tendency to compare our previous successes with our current success. Our audience is an audience of One. And, praise the Lord, He sees it all. Our identity is not based on success at all. Our identity is based on service, the same service that we witness when we read about the early Christians who were called to do hard things. When the pilgrims came from England to North America on the *Mayflower*, they encountered many hardships. Things didn't go as they had planned. They were being obedient to God's calling, but they still suffered through many heartaches. They didn't question God's calling on their life. They didn't quit because their success was not dependent on whether they lived happily ever after. No, their success was defined by whether they came to hear our Father say, "Well done, thou good and faithful servant" (Matthew 25:21). This is what should define our success too.

There are two passages I want to share with you. They both serve as a reminder that if things are going well and we see the fruits of our labor, which is a beautiful testimony for all of us to witness, we must not forget that the Lord is in control of it all. Cherish the fruits. Don't come to expect the fruits. Remember, each day is a gift to be cherished. Be thankful for each gift. Reaping rewards for our labor is not something owed to us. May we keep our focus on Him and live in gratefulness. These passages can help us to keep our eyes on the prize. May we keep these verses in mind:

Deuteronomy 8

> Beware that thou forget not the Lord thy God, in not keeping his commandments, and his judgments, and his statutes, which I command thee this day: Lest when thou hast eaten and art full, and hast built goodly houses, and dwelt

therein; And when thy herds and thy flocks multiply, and thy silver and thy gold is multiplied, and all that thou hast is multiplied; Then thine heart be lifted up, and thou forget the Lord thy God, which brought thee forth out of the land of Egypt, from the house of bondage. (Deuteronomy 8:11–14)

My prayer is that you will always be mindful to remain humble in the calling that the Lord has placed upon your life. May you be thankful for the successes with which the Lord chooses to graciously bless you. Be vigilant in prayer for your family and those families that make up your circle of friends.

Habakkuk 3

Although the fig tree shall not blossom, neither shall fruit be in the vines; the labour of the olive shall fail, and the fields shall yield no meat; the flock shall be cut off from the fold, and there shall be no herd in the stalls: Yet I will rejoice in the Lord, I will joy in the God of my salvation. (Habakkuk 3:17–18)

Lastly, please think on this: These verses do not say that the farmer didn't plant the fig tree or didn't prune the vines. It doesn't say that he didn't weed the crops or didn't care for the sheep. It only says that though they didn't produce what he expected, he still said, "I will still rejoice." He didn't say, "I quit. I'm no longer going to be a farmer," or "I'm no longer going to weed and prune because it doesn't matter whether I do it or not." No. He said, "Yet I will rejoice in the Lord, I will joy in the God of my salvation" (Habakkuk 3:18). You see, his identity did not change. He remained a servant of the Lord.

My prayer is that you do not allow Satan to steal your identity, robbing you of your calling. God knows your heart. He knows your motives. May you be found faithful to Him, knowing that your only identity, the identity that truly defines you, is in Him. May the joy of the Lord be your strength whether things are going as you expected or not. May you be humble in your journey. Be encouraged by the fruit of your labor and the labor of others. May you press on toward the prize, resting in the fact that our Lord sees it all, the whole picture in its entirety, and has a plan. And, praise the Lord, He covers us in grace.

CHAPTER 11

No One Escapes

2 Corinthians 11

Are they ministers of Christ? (I speak as a fool.) I am more; in labours more abundant, in stripes above measure, in prisons more frequent, in deaths oft. (2 Corinthians 11:23)

Reading this passage lets us know that our righteousness is as filthy rags. No one escapes persecution. No one escapes ridicule. If we are to be like Jesus, we will suffer like Jesus. Paul had worked hard for the Lord, *and* he had a past. I am sure he had to ignore many people who would not let him forget where he came from. In order to be usable and to be able to be told, "Well done, good and faithful servant" (Matthew 25:21), you must be willing to see the people who only want to remind you of where you came from and what you have done in the past as deceived people being used by Satan. They are being used by him to take away your joy, to make you feel unworthy and unusable. One of the ways the devil gets a foothold in believers' hearts is by making us believe that if only we hadn't done this, or only if we hadn't acted that way, then we would be usable by God. *Instilling doubt into our witness for Him and destroying our confidence is a tool of Satan.* Paul had committed more atrocities than most of us could ever dream of committing, but he kept his eyes on the prize, pressing forward. He told the Corinthians how he had been in prison, flogged, stoned, and in danger, how he had labored, gone without sleep, and known hunger and thirst, yet daily he faced the concerns of his churches.

My son, you will have many trials in this life. You will face hardships in dealing with people. You will be persecuted for your beliefs. You will have to labor for your family's needs, yet you will still face the daily pressure of concern for your family. You must never let yourself be deceived into thinking, *Well, maybe this person doesn't like those people, but they will like me! They will treat me differently. They will see the goodness in me and like me.* They might, but only for a short time. People can be cruel. You must learn to walk away from those who don't receive you. Don't be determined to get them to like you. That is a quality of pride. If you feel you deserve to be treated fairly because you are kind, then you are saying that you deserve to be treated better than Jesus was treated. He was more than kind. He was love, but He still faced the cross. Know in your heart that people will treat you unkindly no matter what you do. Don't make it your ambition to win them over. Turn it over to the Lord, and wipe your feet off. Continue to live a life pleasing to the Lord. Allow God to love others through you even when there is no love left in your heart for them. Continue to walk in love. Be what God would have you to be: kind, respectful, honest, joyful—because your joy is not based on your circumstances or the people around you. And may you be filled with integrity and honor in your behavior for our Lord. If you are stuck in a situation where you can't move on, such as in a family relationship or a work relationship, this is a time when you have to press on toward the prize, being in continual prayer and seeking to grow in knowledge of Him. Know that your audience is with God, not with man.

CHAPTER 12

Guard Your Heart

Proverbs 4

> Keep thy heart with all diligence; for out of it are
> the issues of life. (Proverbs 4:23)

My precious son, do not be deceived by your own heart or pride, thinking such things as, *I would never do this* or *I would never do that*. The human heart is sinful and produces all manner of evil desires, thoughts, and actions, everything from murder to envy.

We are sinners—saved by grace. We are new creatures once Jesus enters our hearts, but the old nature is still battling for our time, our thoughts, and our actions, as well as our distraction! *Don't be fooled. We cannot change our own nature. Only He can!* We must practice taking every thought captive that does not come from Him. Taking your thoughts captive is a daily exercise for healthy thinking. Honey, every day your eyes and ears will be sent messages through images and expressions that are ungodly. These messages produce impure thoughts. You will be surprised at how quickly you can have ungodly thoughts, attitudes, or pursuits. It takes an inward love fully devoted to our Lord to immediately recognize the evil desires that can spring up in our thought life and to immediately pray for forgiveness and think on things that are pure, lovely, honorable, and praiseworthy. These evil desires spring up in everyone at one time or another. That is why Jesus came to earth, because we all need a Savior. He died for us lost sinners. We are saved by His grace. We have turned our hearts to Him, praise the Lord. We are not in bondage to sin but are set free.

I pray that as you face the many trials that come in this life, you will abstain from all appearances of evil, flee from temptation, and cling to what is pure, right, and holy. "Abstain from *all* appearances of evil" (1 Thessalonians 5:22, emphasis added). This is a discipline in life, and you must train yourself to be on the lookout for all appearances of evil. You must look at things through the eyes of a lost person watching your every action. Is there anything that you are participating in that could be perceived by others in such a way to make them believe that you are *not* who you say you are in Christ? Is there any behavior that you are practicing that could be a stumbling block for a new believer because it does not match up with how a Christian should behave? When you make your daily decisions to agree with others, to speak with others, to participate in activities, and to behave in certain ways, you are making a statement to everyone around you as to how committed you are to the Lord. People are watching, and God is watching. No matter how people may seem, everyone is waiting for a *true* person to come into their lives. They want to find a person to call a friend, a friend whom they can respect and trust. Ultimately we all must place our trust in the Lord, but one way to lead others to Christ is by being a light in this dark and lonely world. If you try to get along with others by acting like them in order to satisfy your own selfish desires to fit in, then you will be like them. Remember, as I have always taught you: be friendly, but that does not mean that the other person is your friend. If it becomes evident to others that you are riding the fence in what you believe, people will eat you alive. People will have no respect for you and will use your behavior as an excuse to treat you even worse. *Respect is earned by being true to your God and yourself from the beginning of a relationship to the end.* If you act one way with one person and another way with another person, then no one will respect or trust you. My son, may you live a life that is honorable, trustworthy, and faithful. Be a man of character, a hard worker, reliable. Be someone who is willing to stand for what is right. Be a man of courage. "True holiness is a matter of inward affection and attitude and not just outward actions and associations."[12]

Son, do not seek the affirmation of man. Do not do things because others are watching or expecting. Do something because it is the right thing to do. Do something because you want to please the Lord. Do something because you are doing it for the Lord, not man. "True worship must come from the heart, and it must be directed by God's truth not man's personal ideas."[13]

---

[12] Mylon LeFevre, "Without Him" (hymn), 1963.

[13] Warren Wiersbe, *Bible Commentary: Old Testament* (Nashville: Thomas Nelson, 1991).

CHAPTER 13

Finish Well

Psalm 27

> Wait on the Lord: be of good courage, and he shall strengthen thine heart: wait, I say, on the Lord. (Psalm 27:14)

My precious son,

This is one of the most difficult things to do, to wait on the Lord. Honey, in times when you are having to wait and things seem senseless, when things seem to be going too far, or when you either experience or witness what you consider to be too much suffering or too many senseless struggles, etc., it is very important to remember that God's ways are not our ways and that His thoughts are not our thoughts. *Being a righteous man of God means not only being willing to stand up for what is right but also having the discipline to wait on God's timing.*

> And the king of Sodom said unto Abram, Give me the persons, and take the goods to thyself.
>
> And Abram said to the king of Sodom, I have lift up mine hand unto the Lord, the most high God, the possessor of heaven and earth,
>
> That I will not take from a thread even to a shoelatchet, and that I will not take any thing that is thine, lest thou shouldest say, I have made Abram rich: (Genesis 14:21-23)

Abram takes a stand for the Lord. When the King of Sodom told Abram to give him the people and keep the goods for himself, Abram boldly responded to his offer by stating, "I have lift up mine hand unto the Lord, the most high God, the possessor of heaven and earth, That I will not take from a thread even to a shoelatchet, and that I will not take any thing that is thine, lest thou shouldest say, I have made Abram rich" (Genesis 14:22–23). Abram wanted to ensure that only the Lord would be glorified.

> The word of the Lord came unto Abram in a vision, saying, Fear not, Abram: I am thy shield, and thy exceeding great reward. (Genesis 15:1)

My son, having the Lord Almighty as your shield is reward enough. The Lord is our shield, our protector, and our provider. This proclamation of love to Abram's heart should have been all the reward and refuge needed to trust in the Lord's provision, but sadly Abram could not rest in this promise. This time, he did not boldly proclaim faith in the Lord, raise his hand to the Lord, and stand on His promises. Instead, he responded, "Lord God, what wilt thou give me, seeing I go childless … to me thou hast given no seed, and, lo, one born in my house is mine heir" (Genesis 15:2–3). The Lord said, "Do not be afraid. I am your shield" (Genesis 15:1). Abram responded with, "What can You give me since You have given me no children?" The boldness we see in Abram's response to the king of Sodom is nowhere to be found in his response to the Lord. In responding to Sodom, he remembered his oath to the Lord, but in his response to the Lord, he did not remember the Lord's promise to him: "I will make you into a great nation" (Genesis 12:2). You see, Abram and his wife were experiencing a heartache that had rattled their faith. Their hearts' desire was to have children. They were getting up in age. When you have a heartache of any kind and years keep passing by without remedy and no end seems near, it is natural for the flesh to focus on the desire and not cling to the promise. We do not naturally patiently wait on the Lord's timing, because His timing is not our timing.

> And, behold, the word of the Lord came unto him, saying, This shall not be thine heir; but he that shall come forth out of thine own bowels shall be thine heir. And he brought him forth abroad, and said, Look now toward heaven, and tell the stars, if thou be able to number them: and he said unto him, So shall thy seed be. And he believed in the Lord; and he counted it to him for righteousness. (Genesis 15:4–6)

The Lord assured Abram of His promise to him. He revealed that his offspring would be as numerous as the stars. Abram believed the Lord.

When the Lord speaks or reveals something to your spouse, He is also speaking to you. The Bible does not say whether or not Abram shared the Lord's revelations with his wife, Sarai, but if he did share this with her, she should have taken this as a promise to her as well. Communication is a beautiful thing in any relationship, but it is extremely important in a marriage. If the Lord reveals something to you or your wife, then the other must always take note of that revelation.

Genesis 16

> Now Sarai Abram's wife bare him no children: and she had an handmaid, an Egyptian, whose name was Hagar. And Sarai said unto Abram, Behold now, the Lord hath restrained me from bearing: I pray thee, go in unto my maid; it may be that I may obtain children by her. And Abram hearkened to the voice of Sarai. And Sarai Abram's wife took Hagar her maid the Egyptian, after Abram had dwelt ten years in the land of Canaan, and gave her to her husband Abram to be his wife. And he went in unto Hagar, and she conceived: and when she saw that she had conceived, her mistress was despised in her eyes. And Sarai said unto Abram, My wrong be upon thee: I have given my maid into thy bosom; and when she saw that she had conceived, I was despised in her eyes: the Lord judge between me and thee. But Abram said unto Sarai, Behold, thy maid is in thine hand; do to her as it pleaseth thee. And when Sarai dealt hardly with her, she fled from her face. (Genesis 16:1–6)

Years passed and still Sarai and Abram had no children. Sarai spoke to Abram and said, "Behold now, the Lord hath restrained me from bearing: I pray thee, go in unto my maid; it may be that I may obtain children by her" (Genesis 16:2). Abram agreed. Once again, he did not react in the same boldness that he had displayed in his response to the king of Sodom. He did not say to his wife, "I have raised my hand to the Lord, God Most High, Creator of heaven and earth, and have believed His promise that our offspring will be as numerous as the stars." No. Having his eyes focused on the heartache and wanting to please his wife, he agreed. She was also fixated on her desire and was determined to fix the problem with what she saw as the only way to humanly fulfill their desire for children. He agreed.

Honey, Abram was a righteous man, yet he still was vulnerable to his wife's desires. Her desire to bear children overrode her desire to wait on the Lord. His desire to please her overrode his desire to trust in the Lord.

If Father Abraham could be enticed to sin in this way, then so can you. This is why you need to be the leader of your household. Be aware of and compassionate toward your wife's emotional desires, but also be firm in what the Lord has called you to do. Lead her lovingly. Make sure her heart is pure and not manipulative before you give your heart to her.

Also, this shows the importance of keeping a prayer journal, so that when you are waiting on the Lord, you may look back and read about times past when God answered your prayers, spoke to your heart, and/or changed your desires to fit with His. Cling to these truths while living day to day in the waiting period of the current trial.

I love you, honey, and I want the best for you and your wife.

CHAPTER 14

Weathering the Storms

My Precious Son,

I want to share with you some passages from God's Word that have helped me to weather the storms of life. The revelation that the Lord has poured into my heart through His Word has given me the strength that I so desperately needed in order to keep going when nothing made sense.

My life verse is, "Let the words of my mouth, and
the meditation of my heart, be acceptable in thy
sight, O Lord, my strength, and my redeemer."
(Psalms 19:14)

At some point, when I was in my twenties, the Lord spoke His
truth into my heart through this verse. I realized that my words
may be pleasing to Him, but was the meditation of my heart
pleasing to Him? No, it was not. I was consumed with the hurts in
my life. I would recount conversations and think of how I should
have responded and what I should have or could have said. I would
imagine future conversations and determine how I would respond
the next time a particular person said something similar again. I
was consumed. I could be in the same room with someone but be
miles away in my mind because I was either reliving a wrong or
imagining a different outcome. There was a lot of "if only" and "I
should have" going on in my mind. The Lord began to convict my
heart of my meditation. He revealed to me that I could not be the
servant that He would have me to be. I could not fulfill the plans
and purposes for my life that He had planned for me if I remained
in this pattern. It was consuming. It took my energy, my patience,
and my time away from His calling upon my life. How could I be
a creative instrument for His glory if I was living in the past or
imagining what I would say next time? So, I sat down and typed
a seven-page letter to the Lord, expressing every hurt and wrong
that was consuming me. I laid these hurts at His feet. I committed
to Him that I would do my very best to take my thoughts captive.
"Casting down imaginations, and every high thing that exalteth
itself against the knowledge of God, and bringing into captivity
every thought to the obedience of Christ" (2 Corinthians 10:5).

You see, I had allowed the wrongs that I had experienced
to become exalted to a higher place than the place where the
Lord was set in my heart and mind. These things that had upset
me, pierced my heart, offended me, etc., were consuming me.

They were taking my joy away. It was as though I could not move on until they had been made right, defended, rectified, etc. But this need for justification was not of the Lord. This ridicule, this bullying, this abuse, whatever you want to call it, was an "excusable" justification for while I was consumed. These wrongs and/or offenses did *not* warrant this so-called "need" of mine to set the record straight or right a wrong. Actually, if I could have replayed every conversation and said exactly what I thought I should have said, it would have only made things worse. It would have escalated the problem. These hurtful conversations had such a high place in my mind that it was causing me not to trust in Him, lean on Him, or recount His promises. I believed that I needed to fix it and vindicate myself in order to be able to move on with my life. It was a problem, and it was unhealthy.

In my letter to the Lord, I promised that if I began to recount a wrong again, I would immediately "cast my care upon Him." The next day, I woke up and prayed for the Lord to help me not think on these things. I asked Him to help me to think only on what was lovely. I quickly found that within an hour I was asking for forgiveness and casting my thoughts. I realized that I needed to break this cycle down slowly, so I asked Him to help me not dwell on these things until 10:00 a.m. Then the length of time during which I would refrain from thinking on these things slowly grew over time, and within a couple of days, I finally made it to lunch without having recounted one conversation. Once I made it to lunch, I would then pray that He would help me keep my mind clear of those thoughts until dinner. If I made it to dinner, I would then pray that He would help me until bedtime. At bedtime, I would pray for the next day. I did this every day, and within two weeks, I was no longer meditating on wrongs and hurts. The Lord healed my heart through this commitment to Him. Praise the Lord, I have never struggled with this sin again. It became such a learned behavior to cast my thoughts and cares onto Him.

I pray that if you become consumed by something that is not

pleasing to the Lord, you will commit your way unto Him and discipline yourself to take every thought captive. Don't let the situation sit on a higher throne in your heart than the throne on which the Lord Jesus Christ sits. For those of us who have trusted in Him as Savior, we have Him on a throne. But both the height of the throne and the place on which the throne sits in our hearts varies. May you never be so consumed with an offense that it becomes greater than the throne He sits on in your heart. Otherwise you will not live a life of abundant joy. Don't let others take your joy. "The joy of the Lord is your strength" (Nehemiah 8:10). If we allow our joy to be taken away, we will no longer be able to be warriors for Him, be creative for Him, or be able to fulfill His plan and purposes for our lives, nor will we be able to live the abundant life He has for us. "Let the words of my mouth, and the meditation of my heart, be acceptable in thy sight, O Lord, my strength, and my redeemer" (Psalm 19:14).

I have truly learned that if I "let the words of my mouth, and the meditation of my heart, be acceptable in His sight," then nothing else matters. He is my audience, and since He is my audience, I am content with His acceptance. I pray that you will be too.

I love you, my son, and I hope you will make it a practice to take your thoughts captive. It is freeing. It is joy.

CHAPTER 15

Sometimes the Journey is Too Much

1 Kings 19

And Ahab told Jezebel all that Elijah had done, and withal how he had slain all the prophets with the sword. Then Jezebel sent a messenger unto Elijah, saying, So let the gods do to me, and more also, if I make not thy life as the life of one of them by to morrow about this time. And when he saw that, he arose, and went for his life, and came to Beersheba, which belongeth to Judah, and left his servant there. But he himself went a day's journey into the wilderness, and came and sat down under a juniper tree: and he requested for himself that he might die; and said, It is enough; now, O Lord, take away my life; for I am not better than my fathers. And as he lay and slept under a juniper tree, behold, then an angel touched him, and said unto him, Arise and eat. And he looked, and, behold, there was a cake baken on the coals, and a cruse of water at his head. And he did eat and drink, and laid him down again. And the angel of the Lord came again the second time, and touched him, and said, Arise and eat; because the journey is too great for thee. (1 Kings 19:1–7)

Here in the Word of the Lord we read how the Lord has His angel tell Elijah, "The journey is too great for thee" (1 Kings 19:7b). My son, sometimes the journey *is* too great for us. Some trials are unbearable, but somehow we keep waking up and going through the motions of life, and unbelievably we make it through a tragedy that seemed as though it would consume us. Many times, well-meaning people will try to encourage you when you are going through a tremendous trial by reciting James: "My brethren, count it all joy when ye fall into divers temptations; knowing this, that the trying of your faith worketh patience" (James 1:2–3). These verses are true, and yes, your faith grows and your endurance becomes evident through trials, but this verse is not always appropriate for the trial that you are encountering. Reading these confirming Words of the Lord, in which the Sovereign Lord recognizes that sometimes the journey is too much for us, is such a comfort.

When Elijah found out that his life was in danger, he ran through the wilderness. When he came to the juniper tree, he sought refuge under it. He rested there. He did not run to others for protection. He did not tell everyone about his troubles. No, he found solace alone, and the Lord met him there. The Lord spoke reassuring words to him there. He was fed by the Lord alone. Sometimes we need to find solace in the Lord alone. Sometimes we need to be fed by Him and Him alone. Sometimes no one else is going to understand what you are going through except the Lord, and that is okay. He is our refuge. He is our Rock. This is not to say that you should not seek others' counsel during trials and tribulations, but some trials require sitting under His covering in the midst of the wilderness and being ministered to and fed by Him and Him alone.

> And he arose, and did eat and drink, and went in the strength of that meat forty days and forty nights unto Horeb the mount of God. (1 Kings 19:8)

The Lord gave Elijah what he needed. The Lord strengthened him. To God be the glory.

> And he came thither unto a cave, and lodged there; and, behold, the word of the Lord came to him, and he said unto him, What doest thou here, Elijah? And he said, I have been very jealous for the Lord God of hosts: for the children of Israel have forsaken thy covenant, thrown down thine altars, and slain thy prophets with the sword; and I, even I only, am left; and they seek my life, to take it away. (1 Kings 19:9–10)

Elijah was still in turmoil. He was still fearful of the outcome. Sometimes when we are facing a trial, we seek the Lord, embrace the Lord, listen to His voice, and again retreat in defeat, submitting to our fear. This is the perfect example of why it is so important to hide the Word of the Lord in your heart. Know the Word.

Recount His mercies. Elijah was now hiding in a cave. His fears had consumed him, but the Lord spoke to him there. The Lord showed Himself to Elijah. O what a mighty Lord we serve!

> And he said, Go forth, and stand upon the mount before the Lord. And, behold, the Lord passed by, and a great and strong wind rent the mountains, and brake in pieces the rocks before the Lord; but the Lord was not in the wind: and after the wind an earthquake; but the Lord was not in the earthquake: And after the earthquake a fire; but the Lord was not in the fire: and after the fire a still small voice. And it was so, when Elijah heard it, that he wrapped his face in his mantle, and went out, and stood in the entering in of the cave. And, behold, there came a voice unto him, and said, What doest thou here, Elijah? And he said, I have been very jealous for the Lord God of hosts: because the children of Israel have forsaken thy covenant, thrown down thine altars, and slain thy prophets with the sword; and I, even I only, am left; and they seek my life, to take it away. And the Lord said unto him, "Go, return on thy way to the wilderness." (1 Kings 19:11–15)

My Dear Son,

These verses mean so much to me. The Lord is asking Elijah, "What are you doing here?" Elijah is feeling as though he is the only one. He may feel that there is no need to return to his life because no one else feels the way he does or understands him. How can he go back to the wilderness and continue to live? The Lord, in His grace, reveals Himself to Elijah.

My son, these verses have healed my heart so much.

*The great and powerful winds came, but the Lord
was not in the wind.*

My daddy's abuse and ugly behavior came, but the Lord was
not in the abuse.

*An earthquake came, but the Lord was not in the
earthquake.*

My daddy was in a mental hospital, and the hospital staff did
not do what needed to be done and let him out. He had threatened
to burn the house down and kill my precious mother, but the Lord
was not in this.

*Then, after the fire, a still small voice. Yes, the still
small voice—this was the Lord!**

Then, after forty years of subjecting us to abuse—which was
escalated during the last nine and a half years of my daddy's life
because of his battle with cancer—at the end of his life, my daddy
was in the ICU. The hospital told us that he was near death and
that we needed to place him into hospice. He sat on the edge of his
bed in the ICU and began to rage at my mom and me for the last
time. As he began, a gentle small voice whispered into my heart
and said, "See, this is all he is capable of. Love him." With that
merciful truth, I was able to love my daddy through his rage, and
not fear. Because, you see, the Lord was in the whisper.

My son, the Lord allowed all of these things to happen because
He gives us free will. If you or a loved one chooses to sin, that
choice is not without consequence. Your sin is not your own. Your
sin affects everyone around you. Sin has consequences. Even if you
are not the one sinning, you cannot live with sin and not feel the
effects of the consequences in your own life. That is evidence of

a just God. The sinner must face the consequences of his sin, and those closest to him will feel the effects. "When you pass through the waters, I will be with you; and when you pass through the rivers, they will not sweep over you. When you walk through the fire, you will not be burned; the flames will not set you ablaze" (Isaiah 43:2). This passage does not say *if* you pass through the waters. No, it says *when*. The waters will come, and you will feel like you are drowning, but He will be with you. The rivers will rise, but they will not drown you. The fire will be hot, but you will not be destroyed by it.

Your choice to sin will cause your family to struggle, and their choice to sin will cause you to struggle. You may be doing your best to live for the Lord, but if you are entangled with someone who is not, you will suffer the consequences of their sin. Choose well, my son.

*My daddy did not burn the house down. He threatened to do so. The use of the word *fire* in this sentence is symbolic of the firestorm in our lives. We were in fear. We experienced an earthquake of shattered emotions. The fire after the earthquake symbolizes, for me, how we dealt with the aftermath of these threats. Once my daddy came back home, we lived each day constantly looking to see if another fire was going to emerge from the rubbish. We lived in fear of what mood he would be in each day. Walking on eggshells was a way of life. We lived continually hoping he was not going to ignite.

My son, this account, in many ways, describes my childhood. It wasn't always this extreme. Each day I woke up wondering what mood my daddy was going to be in that day. It was a roller coaster. It was hard.

I have always told you, and I want to reiterate the fact, that you don't really know someone until you live with them. Please guard your heart. Don't be cynical, but please use wisdom and discernment when you meet people.

My daddy was a different person at church. He was a different person in public. He acted one way with people of the world and tried to be worldly to fit in. He acted another way at church and tried to fit in. Depending on his mood, he would witness to people one time when he encountered them, and then he would tell an inappropriate joke the next time he saw them. There were signs that revealed who he really was, if people were paying attention.

Pay attention. If people are genuine, they remain the same no matter who they are around, no matter their circumstances, and no matter their environment.

A person who is honest, trustworthy, and sincere is one who has the same reputation within all their groups of friends. When their friends from all walks of their life come together and share stories about this person, the person should be recognizable by every friend group. No compartmentalization of behavior should be evident. The person remains the same at home as they are at work, at church, or at play. I have always prayed that you will marry someone who is honest, trustworthy, and sincere. I pray that you will choose a wife who loves the Lord her God with all her heart, soul, and mind. I also pray that you will be honest, trustworthy, and sincere. I pray that you will always love the Lord your God with all your heart, soul, and mind. May you be what you need to be for your wife, and may she be what she needs to be for you. May the Lord bless you both abundantly in your lives. May you both be found faithful.

May the one whom the Lord has set aside for you be found by you. May you be what you need to be for her. May you be an answer to her parents' prayers. May she be what we have prayed for you. May she be an answer to your prayers.

Again I pray: choose well, my son.

Bibliography

BibleGateway.com. 'www.BibleGateway.com' Zondervan.

Butler, Greg. Bible Baptist Church. Sermon Quote. www. biblebapt.org.

Hall, Mark. 'Slow Fade.' Casting Crowns. *The Altar and The Door.* 2007.

LeFevre, Mylon. 'Without Him.' Hymn. 1961.

Stanley, Charles. First Baptist Church of Atlanta. Sermon Quote. www.fca.org.

Wiersbe, Warren, *Bible Commentary Old Testament.* Nashville: Thomas Nelson Publishers, 1991.